Coleridge's Ancient Mariner

Coleridge's Ancient Mariner

AN EXPERIMENTAL EDITION OF
Texts and Revisions 1798-1828

Edited with Commentary by
Martin Wallen

Clinamen Studies
STATION HILL

Published by Station Hill Literary Editions, a project of the Institute for Publishing Arts, Barrytown, New York 12507. Station Hill Literary Editions are supported in part by grants from the National Endowment for the Arts, a Federal Agency in Washington, D.C., and by the New York State Council on the Arts.

Cover design by Susan Quasha.

Distributed by the Talman Company, 131 Spring Street, Suite 201E-N, New York, New York 10012.

Library of Congress Cataloging-in-Publication Data

Coleridge, Samuel Taylor, 1772-1834.
      [Rime of the ancient mariner]
      The ancient mariners of Samuel Taylor Coleridge : the texts of 1798-1828/ edited with commentary by Martin Wallen.
            p. cm.   —   (Clinamen studies)
      Includes bibliographical references.
      ISBN 0-88268-123-0 (cloth): $34.95.—ISBN 0-88268-148-6 (pbk.): $16.95
      1. Coleridge, Samuel Taylor. 1772-1834. Rime of the ancient mariner—Criticism, Textual. I. Wallen, Martin. II. Title. III. Series: Clinamen studies series.
PR4479.A2W34   1993
821'.7—dc20   92-37977
                                                        CIP

Manufactured in the United States of America.

Contents

Foreword

Martin Wallen's edition of Coleridge's "Ancient Mariner" adds a significant page to the unusual publication history of an icon of Romantic poetry and opens entirely new paths of critical perception for reading across the textual boundaries of this remarkable poem. By situating the three primary "versions" of the poem as horizontal strips of typography across the page, this edition takes on the look of a hieroglyphic system or frieze: a spatial orthography that converts the different phases in the poem's production into fragments of near-repetition and, by means of its apparatus of delimiters, foregrounds the minutely particular variations in spelling and punctuation that have been obscured (or repressed) in previous editions of the poem. The graphic configuration of these texts provides a technology for *noticing* patterns of interference that otherwise would go unobserved, resulting in a text that is productively "unreadable" as a continuous narrative. Deploying the texts *vertically* in this way allows the "versions," in effect, to act as mutual glosses on each other, architectonic transformations of the marginal glosses *situated beside* the poem proper, beginning with the 1817 *Sibylline Leaves* edition.

Given the fact that this edition incorporates all variations of the "Mariner" texts through 1828, including Coleridge's handwritten revisions to the poem, as well as so-called printing "errors," the temptation is great to attribute the revisions to Coleridge's "intention," and to assess any textual situation where this intention was not carried out (such as the publisher's inclusion of a stanza describing the mate of Nightmare LIFE-IN-DEATH which Coleridge wanted to have deleted from *Sibylline Leaves*) as a "mistake" that should be corrected in any authoritative edition. In his "Commentary" to the poem, however, Wallen brackets the question of intention and relegates the incessant revisions to the poem to the ontological domain of the tale itself — that is, by its very nature the tale questions its own identity and tempts its readers and interpreters to retell or recreate that lost identity (that never was) in a way that completes it or gains access to its ever-receding origin.

In such a revisionary situation, the boundaries between *textuality* — indeterminate, apparently random or "accidental" texual occurrences (features which "show up" in the process of production) — and *intentionality* — determinate, necessary, presumably conscious meaning — begin to overlap and blur. The conflict between textuality and intentionality permeates every level of this poem and parallels the differences between the poem's narrative proper and the marginal glosses. The tale itself insists on the intertwining at every moment of an absolute uncertainty with an absolute determinacy in which one thing simply happens after another, yet seems driven by a hidden inevitability (witness especially the dice game discussed below). By contrast, the gloss voice is never uncertain, never expresses a doubt — it is a voice of metaphysical stability and foundationalism, of certainty, absoluteness, complete decidability, and causal connectedness. Yet unlike the poem whose lines are anchored to rhyming end-stops, the glosses exhibit typographic fluidity, making the placement of words and line breaks appear accidental, random, contingent, and optional, creating an opposition between the visible, typographic form and the rhetorical stability of the glosses.

In this form the text has far-reaching implications for reading Coleridge and Romanticism in general. The apparatus of Wallen's edition reveals how the 1805 edition drastically normalizes Coleridge's deviant use of quotation marks in 1798 (slightly less so in 1800) in order to keep all the printed voices in the poem — especially the narrator's and the Mariner's — meticulously distinct from one another. The "Commentary" suggests Wordsworth's culpability for the normalized 1805 edition and calls attention to Coleridge's reversal of most of the normalizations regarding the Mariner's voice when he regained control over the poem in 1817. No other currently available edition reveals the crisis of voice as it is textualized through the presence, absence, and situation of quotation marks in the different incarnations of the poem.

In the E. H. Coleridge edition, on which many anthologized versions of the poem are based, quotation marks cease to enclose the Mariner's speech immediately after the first appearance of the word "Moon-shine," making the confession — ["]With my cross-bow / I shot the ALBATROSS["] — typographically undifferentiated from the third person narrator who opens the poem. Any critic who takes such graphic marks seriously is tempted to draw sweeping conclusions from this apparent textual slip — for example, that "Coleridge" is unable to keep the teller of the tale and the teller of the telling of the tale separate precisely at the point where the confession occurs, suggesting that *the telling of the tale itself is somehow the primary act of transgression that violates the fiction of separate voices*. Wallen's edition shows that there is no authorial justification for attributing the disappearance of quotation marks from this point on to "S. T. Coleridge" since it appears in no edition published during his lifetime. Nevertheless, this textual effect persists in all printings of the poem that follow E.H. Coleridge's edition — a text which especially disguises this minute detail of the poem's history since it accurately reproduces the aberrant punctuation of the 1798 edition in an appendix. Although this discrepancy — which in many ways yields a more interesting reading than S.T. Coleridge's own — is probably attributable to a decision by J. D. Campbell, on whose edition "E. H. Coleridge" based his own, and thus may be explained as a printing "error" that got iterated, this discrepancy occupies the margin between textuality and intentionality, since it is a property of the text's history that emerged directly from Coleridge's intentions to problematize textual voice even though it is something that S.T. Coleridge never authorized.

That S.T. Coleridge was vitally concerned with the role of these tiny punctuation marks is amply demonstrated by the "Commentary" to this edition as well as by the visual juxtaposition of the texts themselves, which allows certain facts to leap into full view. In the 1798 edition, the narrator and the Mariner are not distinguished whatsoever by marks of punctuation, and most statements by other characters (such as the Wedding-Guest and the Hermit) are marked by open quotation marks only and are rarely closed (indeed, close quotation marks are the anomaly and call attention to themselves). The 1805 edition unequivocally stabilizes all vocal distinctions (with one apparent slip [the missing close quotation mark of the Spirit's speech at line 443 in this edition]). In *Sibylline Leaves*, quotation marks surround the Mariner's utterance of "There was a ship"; then they reopen the Mariner's tale at line 21 and finally close it at the end of line 621, technically sub-embedding all subsequent statements — including the Wedding-Guest's — in the Mariner's own voice (which in turn is embedded within the narrator's voice). The most crucial anomaly that

shows up in the twentieth century for the first time in Wallen's text, however — one
which haunts the 1828 edition (as well as the 1834 edition, whose differences
Wallen does not include) — is the set of quotation marks that stand at the end of
line 621 to mark the conclusion of the Mariner's speech: these marks close a
quotation that never officially opened, since in these editions *there are no marks
to open the Mariner's speech at line 21 as there was in 1817*. Logically, at the
end of the tale the Mariner's voice *should* be typographically distinguished from
the narrator's, since the poem starts out that way. Surprisingly, instead of adding
quotation marks to line 21 (as in 1817), the widely anthologized modern editions
of the poem decline to place close quotation marks at the end of the Mariner's
speech — despite their presence in 1817, 1828, and 1834 — as if the apparent
"mistake" of missing quotation marks (apparently initiated by Campbell's
situating close quotation marks after "Moon-shine") had become canonized
despite its illogicality. To see this anomaly as no more than a printing error that
repeats an incorrect decision by the author is to disregard how the poem's textual
history has enacted the problem of who is speaking and when the speaking is
happening that Wordsworth was so anxious to eradicate from the 1805 edition.
The "error" became possible because "Coleridge" called into question the
difference between narrative voices in the first place, a textual situation which
then (as was often the case) moved beyond his control.

Nowhere are the interferences between textuality and intentionality more
urgent than in the famous dice game that occupies one of the poem's epicenters.
The textual revisions that occur in the vicinity of this sequence show up in a new
way when viewed in light of this edition. In its attempt to fill in informational
gaps in the poem, the marginal gloss at this point both *substitutes for deleted
material* in earlier stages of the text and *interacts with the revisions themselves*.
"Night-Mair LIFE-IN-DEATH" is first named in the 1817 edition, and the gloss
explaining that the Mariner is her prize tells so much more than the poem proper
and so significantly much more than it knows it is telling that most readers
remember the information in this gloss as part of the poem proper. (To the extent
that its interpretation is borne out by the ensuing narrative events, the gloss seems
to be anticipating something that makes the future of the poem coherent. The only
other time LIFE-IN DEATH shows up is in a future gloss.) Because the gloss itself

refers to "Life-in-Death" by name this gloss exists *only in relation to this state of the text*:

The naked hulk alongside came,	Death, and Life-in-Death have diced for the ship's crew and she (the latter) winneth the ancient Mariner.
And the twain were casting dice;	
"The game is done, I've, I've won"	
Quoth she, and whistles thrice.	

On the one hand, the dice game is random, a game of pure chance, and is thus aligned with the indeterminacy of textual happenings; on the other hand, the outcome of the game is absolutely determined, in that, *if the gloss is correct*, the game could have come out no other way. *Any other way would have been no way*, for, according to the gloss, if Death had won the Mariner, there would be no tale. But this bind is precisely what is *called into existence* by the gloss's filling in the direct object of "won" in the poem proper.

In addition, in all earlier versions of the poem it was very clear that the woman's mate was male — "*His* bones were black," etc. (in fact, in 1798 the word "mate" does not even occur but rather the masculine "fleshless Pheere" [180]). In the 1817 edition, however, Coleridge "intended" that every stanza describing the "woman's mate" be deleted (which effectively would have deleted all reference to this figure's gender). The strength of Coleridge's desire for this revision is clear from his fury at the publisher for leaving in the stanza describing this "other" figure (see p. 33, n. 36). Though it is by no means clear that Coleridge wanted the stanza deleted *because* it retained the masculine features of the mate, this is unquestionably one effect the deletion produces. The gloss refers to the mate unequivocally as "Death," but the poem proper only *asks* if the figure is "a Death." One of the most crucial points here is the seemingly innocuous parenthetical statement "(the latter)"; if Death is male (as the woman's companion clearly was in earlier editions), why does the gloss need to specify that "she" ("Life-in-Death") is "the latter"? The poem proper makes it absolutely clear that Life-in-Death is female ("The Night-Mair Life-in-Death was she / Who thicks man's blood with cold"). In an apparent attempt to leave no doubt concerning which of these figures won the game, the gloss actually brings into question the gender of the figure who is no longer gendered in the text but who was gendered in the earlier versions of the text, and gendered quite extensively as a male counterpart to the female.

For example, *her* and *his* are italicized in the earlier editions, emphasizing the sexual difference of the two figures, as they emerge from the neuter "it" the mariner first sees and as *"her"* migrates from describing the ship to describing the woman: "Are those *her* sails....Are those *her* ribs....*Her* lips were red, *her* looks were free" in contrast to *"His* bones were black with many a crack, / All black and bare, I ween / Jet black and bare...." (The text retains the italics on *her* even after all trace of the masculine other has been effaced from the poem.) A line from an unpublished stanza emphasizes the gender difference even more decisively: "The Woman and a fleshless Man" (line 189 in this edition). Lines 199-202 of *Sibylline Leaves*, the stanza whose inclusion angered Coleridge so, also leaves no doubt as to the gender of the "woman's mate": "A gust of wind sterte up behind / And whistled through his bones; / Through the holes of his eyes and the hole of his mouth, / Half whistles and half groans." Yet vestiges of a (negative) feminine haunt these descriptions of the masculine mate: "crack," "ween" (homophonic with "wean"), "mouldy damps," and "holes." Even the woman's whistling thrice seems to be analyzed in the (deleted) image of the wind whistling through exactly three holes in her mate's head. Whatever reasons Coleridge may have had for wanting these descriptions deleted, one thing that ends up missing here by virtue of these deletions is precisely an acknowledgement of the gender of the mate, which then, in Coleridge's perverse addition, is called into question by a gloss that attempts to answer *another* question — namely, not *who* is speaking the words, "I've won," about which there seems to be no question in the poem, but rather *what this statement means*: "She (the latter) winneth the ancient Mariner."

In the 1798 edition, the ship is twice referred to as "naked" (*"her* naked ribs" [177] and "The naked hulk" [202]). The gloss, "Like vessel, like crew!" which, by its position in the margin seems to be commenting on LIFE-IN-DEATH only, carries with it the suggestion that both figures aboard the ship are female and "naked" as well (the proximity of this gloss to the word "naked" in fact shows up in the Modern Library edition of the poem, where "Like vessel, like crew!" stands directly beside the words, "The naked hulk").

The possibility, or logically the necessity in terms of the gloss's clarifica-
tions — "Like vessel, like crew!" and "she (the latter)" — that both figures are
female, naked, and (potentially, if not primarily, sexual) "mates" on the ship
whose ribs imprison the masculine sun (1817: 185-86) permit a glimpse of more
controversial aspects of the poem. If the woman and her mate are both female,
then the interaction of the glosses with the revisions converts this textual event
into a primal scene fantasy. This is the moment when the Mariner is born into his
own future by the (sexual) mating of two ghastly females, suggesting a deep but
displaced revulsion from and attraction to female homosexuality (a narrative
feature that underwrites much of "Christabel" as well). Narratively, this is the
moment where the frame story of the marriage feast gets turned inside out. The
Mariner (as mediated through the gloss) is fixated on two textually veiled
females, DEATH and LIFE-IN-DEATH, mating at the crucial dice game, which itself
marries chance and necessity. The poem also feeds into the counter-movement
to homophobia — the underlying homosexual implications of the Mariner's
"lesson." Though this "Foreword" is not the appropriate place to go into detail,
it might suffice to note a few key points. The Mariner tells his tale only to males
("The moment that his face I see / I know the man who must hear me / To him
my tale I teach" [592-94]); he first tells his tale to the Hermit who also relates
only to men and whose place of kneeling is described in graphic terms that
emphasize precisely what is "wholly hid[den]" — "the rotted old oak stump,"
(1798, 566-70; 1800 and 1817, 524-27) a complex (and apparently gratuitous)
detail that conjures up the stump of the tree from which the cross was made (the
"rood," interjected into all three versions [p. 75]) as a not-so-veiled castration
image; and the result of the Mariner's teaching is to turn the Wedding-Guest from
the Bridegroom's door. In this context, the scene in which the Mariner suppos-
edly undergoes redemptive transformation when he blesses the water-snakes
(which appear in this form only at this point in the poem) becomes excessively
problematic. The powerfully ambivalent associations snakes have in Christian
and non-Christian myths raise the issue of what it is the Mariner is committing
himself to. The "hoary flakes" that fall from the snakes in the light of the moon
(1798:279; 1800:283; 1817:280) recall the leprous-like white skin (1798:198,
1800:189; 1817:192) of Night-mair LIFE-IN-DEATH. In addition, the homophobic
and homosexual dimensions of the poem (which I am merely hinting at here),

especially as the text turns on the scenes with the dice game and with the snakes, calls into question the apparent "Christian" foundation of the tale as it radiates from the domain of the wedding — which is a sacrament of the church, the lawful means of heterosexual intercourse and reproduction, and a reigning metaphor for the apocalyptic promise of Christianity (the account in Revelation of the Church as the Bride of Christ, as transformed from the erotic imagery of the Song of Songs).

Moving outward from such textual details to the larger context of the narrative makes it possible to see ways in which the Christian framework *produces* the schizophrenic nature of this divided text rather than *resolves* the textual oppositions that drive the narrative forward. It suddenly makes sense that Christ's name is uttered as an interjection only in the context of disgusting or disturbing events ("The very deep did rot; O! Christ!" [p.22]; "And Christ would take no pity on / My soul in agony" [1798, 1800, p. 39]; "I looked upon the rotting deck; O! Christ! what saw I there"[?]! [p.74]); that the bloody sun brings no salvation; that Night-mair Life-in-Death immediately appears as if a response to the Mariner's parenthetical plea to the Virgin Mary ("Heaven's Mother send us grace"); that a white feminine moon presides over the Mariner's blessing of the snakes; that this moon, Night-mair Life-in-Death, and the Virgin Mary — all females — fill in the gaps left in the narrative by the fleeting appearances of the blushing bride ("red as a rose" [and red as the bloody sun?]) whose wedding brackets the tale.

The minute textual details that this new edition foregrounds lead us to ask some very large and disturbing questions: to what extent does the "Mariner" derive its power from a covert participation in both homosexuality and homophobia? To what extent are the Christian beliefs (which Coleridge elsewhere overtly affirms) *the problem rather than the solution*? To what extent might Coleridge be addressing textually, though perhaps unintentionally, the failure of the Christian paradigm — or, more radically, exposing its constitutive role in deforming culture through an apparently benevolent but thoroughly patriarchal message — "*He* prayeth best...."

Of course, questions such as these do not arise purely out of this edition itself but out of a critical atmosphere in which the existence of such an edition has become welcome. Recent shifts in editorial practice, led by critics like Jerome McGann, that have made this edition recognizable and usable have emerged at the point in critical history where textual deconstruction is taken as a natural (even passé) condition and historical inquiry has begun to recognize the full implications of the interpreter's participation in and re-enactment of the object of inquiry. Whereas Coleridge's "Mariner" stood out in the early nineteenth century as a radical impertinence, an incommensurable text that needed to be tamed, Wallen's "Mariner" can celebrate its unreadable intrusion into (and revision of) a critical tradition that has too easily believed that Coleridge knew what he believed.

Donald Ault
Gainsville, Florida

Preface

In Dürer's woodcut, "Knight, Death, and Devil," the Knight who is no longer young rides insouciantly while being stalked by Death and the Devil. The outfitting of the Knight is splendid, showing a careful attention to every detail of the armor, as well as the tack of the horse(who is noticeably shod, in contrast to the other horse). The Knight's plumpness bespeaks a comfortable life, suggesting that his accoutrements have something other than a merely martial significance. The stately, prancing gait of the horse, along with the erect posture of the Knight and the preponderance of vertical lines throughout the picture, emphasizes that the Knight feels no urgency.

In contrast, the two figures whom the Knight is passing indicate that his self-possession is misplaced. The noseless figure holds up a half-empty hourglass, corresponding to the Knight's middle age. This same figure wears a crown, which poses a curious contrast with the broken unshod nag he rides bridled with rope. The crown might suggest a former glory, like the Knight's but now lost; or it might signify that he rules over all that is not comfortable and pleasant, like the two snakes that have entwined themselves about his crown and his neck. The horned figure who follows the Knight is a study in gruesomeness: while the crowned figure has no nose and no lips, this one has only too much of both, with a snaggle-toothed pig's snout and wattles. The single horn atop his head, along with his cross-eyed gaze, indicates an idiocy that would be comical were it not matched with the twisted horns behind the ears, the cloven hooves, and the rat-like tail just visible inside the frame, all of which suggest a gross brutality. With his barbed right paw, he reaches toward the Knight as though to grab him unawares.

Like the two gruesomes trying to waylay the Knight, the state of the forest does not suggest a pleasant environment. The blasted trees in the background to the right and the large piece of slate to the left suggest disease and decay, corresponding to the skull behind Dürer's framed signature. Only the castle on the mountain-top seems pleasant. But the Knight seems to care for it no more than for the two figures accosting him.

The stark contrasts in this scene, the apparent iconological significance of all the details, lend the engraving a most fascinating power. In this way the scene serves as an almost exact parallel with "The Ancient Mariner," which has commanded a widely ranging fascination since its first inception, both from Coleridge as well as from his audiences. Like Dürer's engraving, Coleridge's poem seems to present a straightforward allegory of the man who should pay closer attention to his surroundings. But, because Coleridge revised the poem at least five times, the allegorical significance of the poem as a whole, as well as the iconological significance of individual details, shifts repeatedly, even to the point of contradiction.

Perhaps instead of forging a parallel between Dürer's engraving and Coleridge's poem, we should instead read the engraving as an allegory of the scholarly tradition which has read "The Ancient Mariner" with so much insouciance. Without seriously questioning the stability of Coleridge's texts, scholarship has placed them firmly in the great tradition of humanist letters. Heavily armored, scholarship has yet to turn its head to meet the most serious challenges awaiting it. Or perhaps scholarship does not ride the mount at all: perhaps the better image is the dog who rushes to seize the skull noticed by only one other figure in the scene, the broken nag.

For this edition of "The Ancient Mariner," I have relied on the six published versions of the poem which appeared in Coleridge's lifetime. I have divided these versions chronologically into three groups, beginning in each case with the first version of the particular period. The three periods are demarcated thus: the first appearance of the poem in the anonymous publication of *Lyrical Ballads* in 1798; the second appearance of the poem in the 1800 edition of *Lyrical Ballads*; the first publication of the poem under Coleridge's name in *Sibylline Leaves* in 1817.

The 1798 division represents the versions of the poem which appeared in the first edition of *Lyrical Ballads* in two separate releases — the first by Biggs and Cottle, the second by J. and A. Arch. The two releases are virtually identical, apart from incidental details altered after publication, and Coleridge's marginal emendations.

The 1800 division represents the poem as it appeared in the two-volume version of *Lyrical Ballads* of 1800, and as it passed through two more editions of 1802 and

1805. Coleridge made numerous revisions for the 1800 edition, and then a considerable number of further revisions appeared in 1802 and 1805.

The 1817 division represents the poem as it appeared in the collection of Coleridge's poems, *Sibylline Leaves*, and includes the variants appearing in the 1828 *Poetical Works*, as well as those in the notebooks. Since this latter edition contains the last version of the poem which appeared in Coleridge's lifetime, the inclusion of texts stops here.

The alterations which appear in each of the chronological periods are marked with brackets. The list of Abbreviations and Symbols indicates the significance of all the brackets and should be consulted in any study of the revisions.

In the following edition I have not sought to provide a readable text of the poem; nor have I followed the conventional editorial principle that the final version overseen by an author in his lifetime constitutes the authoritative form. In fact I have sought to avoid allowing any version to achieve privilege over any other, to prevent the suggestion of a final, authoritative text. The three divisions I have made are primarily chronological, and dependant on the occurrence of a large number revisions altering the shape of the text significantly. Thus, the first sizeable revision occurred for the 1800 version with the deletion of several stanzas, and the next sizeable one occurred with the addition of the gloss for the 1817 version. The aim of the present edition is to identify all the variants which occurred between 1798 and 1828, without privileging one version over another. The result of this aim has been that even changes generally considered incidental have been included, such as punctuation or the inclusion of the participial "e" in a word like "cleared."

This edition does not purport to be a facsimile of any of the six versions. Thus certain limitations arise as to the representation of details of a particular version, such as the title page. These are indicated in the footnotes. Nor does this edition pretend to be a variorum, as none of the variants of editions published after 1828 has been signified. These editions include the 1834 edition, which Coleridge was working on at the time of his death, as well as those published by Sara Coleridge, Richard Garnett, J. D. Campbell, or E. H. Coleridge. The guiding principle of this edition is simply to lay bare the compulsive nature of Coleridge's revision of this poem.

The Commentary following the text of the poem attempts three things: to provide some historical background to Coleridge's numerous revisions; to show what this edition discloses about "The Ancient Mariner" in particular; and to indicate how the compulsiveness of the textual revisions arises from a dominant theme of the Mariner's narration. By no means does the discussion offered in the Commentary purport to be conclusive, but is intended only to indicate the general problems contained in the textual history of this particular poem.

Many different people have supported me in this project, which is a fact that speaks strongly of the need for such an edition of this poem. I am grateful to the Master and Fellows of Trinity College Cambridge for allowing me to print Coleridge's marginal revisions from the copies of *Lyrical Ballads* in their possession. I have also relied on copies of *Lyrical Ballads* in the British Library; these texts, as well as Add MS 47508 f9 from the notebooks, appear here by permission of the British Library. My thanks go to Dr. D. P. Waley of the Manuscripts Room, and to Mr. J. P. W. Gaskell for their kind help. Darla Miller provided me patient and expert technical assistance, and Baekyun Yoo diligently tracked down my errors. Linda Austin read through all the drafts of the Commentary and offered both advice and boundless support. The guidance given me by Don Ault has shaped my understanding not only of this poem and of Coleridge, but of literature in general. Charles Shepherdson first suggested to me that such a project might be done, and he has continued to prove more than a friend throughout the years. Some of the most recent critical developments, in England and America, were brought to my attention by Kevin Jackson whose acumen is always a refreshment to me; of his diligence I can promise, it was worth it.

Special thanks to the Deans of Oklahoma State University, who provided the generous financial support for publication of this book.

Abbreviations and Symbols

Campbell	*The Poetical Works of Samuel Taylor Coleridge.* Ed. James Dykes Campbell. London: Macimillan, 1896.
EHC	*Poetical Works of Samuel Taylor Coleridge.* Ed. E.H. Coleridge. Oxford:Oxford University Press, 1912.
Garnett	*The Poetry of Samuel Taylor Coleridge.* Ed. Richard Garnett New York: Charles Scribner's Sons, 1898.
Griggs	*The Collected Letters of Samuel Taylor Coleridge.* Ed. Earl Leslie Griggs. Oxford: Oxford University Press. 6 volumes.
Hutchinson	*Lyrical Ballads.* Ed. Thomas Hutchinson. London, 1898.
Johnson	Johnson, Mary Lynn. "How Rare is a 'Unique Annotated Copy of *Sibylline Leaves?*'" *Bulletin of the New York Public Library,* 1979.
LB	*Lyrical Ballads.*
Lowes	Lowes, John Livingstone. *The Road to Xanadu: A Study in the Way of the Imagination.* Revised Edition. London: Macmillan, 1932.
CN	*Notebooks of Samuel Taylor Coleridge.*Ed. Kathleen Coburn, and Bart Winer. Princeton: Princeton University Press, 1957-. 4 volumes to date.
SL	*Sibylline Leaves.*
YSL	Proof copy of *Sibylline Leaves* now in Yale University Library.

1798   *Lyrical Ballads.* Bristol, 1798; Second Issue, London, 1798.

1800   *Lyrical Ballads.* London, 1800, 2 volumes.

1802   *Lyrical Ballads.* London, 1802, 2 volumes.

1805   *Lyrical Ballads.* London, 1805, 2 volumes.

1817   *Sibylline Leaves.* 1817.

1828   *The Poetical Works of Samuel Taylor Coleridge.* London, 1828, 2 volumes.

\\   Variants appearing only in the 1800 edition of Lyrical Ballads.

{}   Variants appearing in Coleridge's letter to Biggs and Cottle (in Griggs), though not in any published text.

[]   Variants peculiar to both the 1802 and the 1805 editions of *Lyrical Ballads.*

<>   Variants peculiar only to the 1805 edition of *Lyrical Ballads.*

//   Variants peculiar to the 1828 *Poetical Works*, though not to the 1817 *Sibylline Leaves.*

|| Variants peculiar to the 1817 *Sibylline Leaves*, though not to the 1828 *Poetical Works.*

Note: Throughout the text, "–<e>d" and "–/e/d" signify replacement of "–ed" for "–'d" in 1805 and 1828 respectively. Delimiters around capital letters signify a   capital letter only in the text corresponding to the particular set of delimiters.

The Texts
of
The Ancient Mariner

1798

THE RIME OF THE ANCYENT MARINERE,
In Seven Parts.

Argument.

How a Ship having passed the Line was driven by Storms to the cold Country towards the South Pole; and how from thence she made her course to the Tropical Latitude of the Great Pacific Ocean; and of the strange things that befell; and in what manner the Ancyent Marinere came back to his own Country.[1]

1800

The Ancient Mariner
A Poet's Reverie.[2]

ARGUMENT.

\How a Ship, having first sailed to the Equator was driven by Storms to the cold Country towards the South Pole; how the Ancient Mariner cruelly, and in contempt of the laws of hospitality, killed a Sea-bird;[3] and how he was followed by many and strange Judgements: {till having finished this penance[4]} and in what manner he came back to his own Country.\

1817

THE RIME OF THE ANCIENT MARINER
In Seven Parts

Facile credo, plures esse Naturas invisibiles quam visibiles in rerum universitate. Sed horum omnium familiam quis nobis enarrabit? et gradus et cognationes et discrimina et singulorum munera? Quid agunt? quæ loca habitant? Harum rerum notitiam semper ambivit ingenium humanum, nunquam attigit. Juvat, interea, non diffiteor, quandoque in animo, tanquam in tabulâ, majoris et melioris mundi imaginem contemplari: ne mens assuefecta hodierniæ vitæ minutiis se contrahat nimis, & tota subsidat in pusillas cogitationes. Sed veritati interea invigilandum est, modusque servandus, ut certa ab incertis, diem a nocte, distinguamus.--T. Burnet: *Archæol. Phil.* p. 68.[5]

---

[1] The Argument appears on what is page 3, the text of the poem begins on page 5.
[2] The half-title page in 1802 contains the subtitle, "A Poet's Reverie," though the heading on the first page of the text, 145, does not; likewise 1805.
[3] R.C. Bald identifies a marginal revision in a copy of 1800 *LB* signed by Coleridge. The last clause of the argument beginning with, "and how," is crossed out, a caret placed before "and," with the following passage written below: "the Spirit, who loved the Sea-bird pursuing him & his Companions, & sh[ ] upagainst them two Spectres; and ho[w] all his Companions perished, & he wa[s] left alone in the becalmed Vessel; ho[w] a choir of Angels descended, and entered into the bodies of the men who died; and in what manner he ca[me] back to his own Country" (*TLS* 26 July 1934: 528). The brackets designate where the text has been damaged in binding.
[4] "Struck out in the MS" (Griggs' note, I:598).
[5] In *SL* the quotation from Burnet appears on page 2, that is, the page facing the one on which the title appears and the poem begins.

1798

I.

It is an ancyent Marinere,
  And he stoppeth one of three:
"By thy long grey beard and thy glittering eye
  "Now wherefore stoppest me?

"The Bridegroom's doors are open'd wide,   5
  "And I am next of kin;
"The Guests are met, the Feast is set, —
  "May'st hear the merry din.

1800

I.

It is an ancient Mariner,
  And he stoppeth one of three:
"By thy long grey⁶ beard and thy glittering eye
  (")Now wherefore stoppest me?

                                          5
(")The Bridegroom's doors are open<e>d wide,
  (")And I am next of kin;
(")The Guests are met, the Feast is set, —
  (")May'st hear the merry din.["]

1817

<table>
<tr>
<td>An ancient
Mariner
meeteth three
Gallants bid-
den to a wed-
ding-feast,
and detaineth
one.</td>
<td>IT is an ancient Mariner,
And he stoppeth one of three.
"By thy long grey beard and glittering eye,
"Now wherefore stopp'st thou me?

"The Bridegroom's doors are open/e/d wide,
"And I am next of kin;
"The guests are met, the feast is set:
"May'st hear the merry din."</td>
<td>5</td>
</tr>
</table>

---

⁶ 1805 prints "gray."

1798

But still he holds the wedding-guest —
  There was a Ship, quoth he —   10
"Nay, if thou'st got a laughsome tale,
"Marinere! come with me."

He holds him with his skinny hand,
  Quoth he, there was a Ship —
"Now get thee hence, thou grey-beard Loon!   15
"Or my Staff shall make thee skip.

1800

But still he holds the wedding<->guest —
  <">There was a Ship,<"> quoth he —   10
"Nay, if thou'st got a laughsome tale,
(")Mariner! come with me."

He holds him with his skinny hand,
  Quoth he, <">There was a Ship — <">
"Now get thee hence, thou grey-beard[7] Loon! 15
(")Or my Staff shall make thee skip.<">

1817

He holds him with his skinny hand,
"There was a ship," quoth he,
"Hold off! unhand me, grey-beard loon!"   10
Eftsoons his hand dropt he.

---

[7] 1805 prints "gray."

1798

He holds him with his glittering eye —
  The wedding guest stood still
And listens like a three year's child;
  The Marinere hath his will.   20

The wedding-guest sate on a stone,
  He cannot chuse but hear:
And thus spake on that ancyent man,
  The bright-eyed Marinere.

1800

He holds him with his glittering eye —
  The wedding<->guest stood still
And listens like a three year(')s<> child;
  The Mariner hath his will.   20

The wedding-guest sate on a stone,
  He cannot chuse[8] but hear:
And thus spake on that ancient man,
  The bright-eyed Mariner.

1817

The wedding-guest is spell-bound by the eye of the old sea faring man, and constrained to hear his tale.

He holds him with his glittering eye —
  The wedding-guest stood still,
And listens like a three years child:
  The Mariner hath his will.   15

The wedding-guest sat on a stone:
  He can not chuse but hear;
And thus spake on that ancient man,
  The bright-eyed mariner.   20

---

[8] 1805 prints "choose."

1798

The Ship was cheer'd, the Harbour clear'd—   25
  Merrily did we drop
Below the Kirk, below the Hill,
  Below the Light-house top.

The Sun came up upon the left,
  Out of the Sea came he: 30
And he shone bright, and on the right
  Went down into the Sea.

1800

<">The Ship was cheer<e>d, the Harbour clear<e>d—   25
  Merrily did we drop
Below the Kirk, below the Hill,
  Below the Light-house top.

The Sun came up upon the left,
  Out of the Sea came he: 30
And he shone bright, and on the right
  Went down into the sea.

1817

|"|The ship was cheer/e/d, the harbour clear/e/d,
Merrily did we drop
Below the kirk, below the hill,
Below the light-house top.

The Sun came up upon the left,   The Mariner   25
Out of the sea came he|;|/!/   tells how the
And he shone bright, and on the right   ship sailed
Went down into the sea.   southward
                                            with a good
                                            wind and fair
                                            weather, till
                                            it reached the
                                            line.

1798

Higher and higher every day,
  Till over the mast at noon—
The wedding-guest here beat his breast,   35
  For he heard the loud bassoon.

The Bride hath pac'd into the Hall,
  Red as a rose is she;
Nodding their heads before her goes
  The merry Minstralsy.   40

1800

Higher and higher every day,
  Till over the mast at noon—<">
The wedding-guest here beat his breast,   35
  For he heard the loud bassoon.

The Bride hath pac<e>d into the Hall,
  Red as a rose is she;
Nodding their heads before her go(es)
  The merry Minstralsy.[9]   40

1817

Higher and higher every day,
  Till over the mast at noon—   30
The Wedding-Guest here beat his breast,
  For he heard the loud bassoon.

The wedding-
guest heareth
the bridal
music; but
the mariner
continueth
his tale.

The bride hath paced into the hall,
Red as a rose is she;
Nodding their heads before her goes   35
The merry minstrelsy.

---

[9] 1805 prints "minstrelsy."

1798

> The wedding-guest he beat his breast,
>   Yet he cannot chuse but hear:
> And thus spake on that ancyent Man,
>   The bright-eyed Marinere.
>
> Listen, Stranger! Storm and Wind,   45
>   A Wind and Tempest strong!
> For days and weeks it play'd us freaks—
>   Like Chaff we drove along.

1800

> The wedding-guest he beat his breast,
>   Yet cannot chuse[10] but hear:
> And thus spake on that ancient Man,
>   The bright-eyed Mariner(.)<:>
>
> <">But now the Northwind[11] came more fierce,[12]   45
>   There came a Tempest strong!
> And Southward still for days and weeks
>   Like Chaff we drove along.

1817

> The Wedding-Guest he beat his breast,
>   Yet he can not chuse but hear;
> And thus spake on that ancient man,
>   The bright-eyed Mariner.   40

The ship
drawn by a
storm toward
the south pole.

> And now the STORM-BLAST came, and he
>   Was tyrannous and strong:
> He struck with his o'ertaking wings,
>   And chased us south along.

---

[10] 1805 prints "choose."

[11] 1805 prints "North wind."

[12] In the letter to Biggs and Cottle, Coleridge first instructed that this line should read, "And now there came the stormy Wind," but cancelled this line for the above (Griggs I:598). The rest of the stanza was to read as in 1798.

1798

Listen, Stranger! Mist and Snow,
  And it grew wond'rous cauld: 50
And Ice mast-high came floating by
  As green as Emerauld.

1800

And now there came both Mist and Snow,
  And it grew wond(')rous cold: 50
And Ice mast-high came floating by
  As green as Emerald.

1817

With sloping masts and dipping prow,   45
As who pursued with yell and blow
Still treads the shadow of his foe
And forward bends his head,
The ship drove fast, loud roar/e/d the blast,
And southward aye we fled.   50

And now there came both mist and snow,
And it grew wondrous cold:
And ice, mast-high, came floating by,
As green as emerald.

1798

> And thro' the drifts the snowy clifts
>   Did send a dismal sheen;
> Ne shapes of men ne beasts we ken —   55
>   The Ice was all between.
>
> The Ice was here, the Ice was there,
>   The Ice was all around:
> It crack'd and growl'd, and roar'd and howl'd —
>   Like noises of a swound,   60

1800

> And thro<ugh> the drifts the snowy clifts
>   Did send a dismal sheen;
> Nor shapes of men nor beasts we ken —   55
>   The Ice was all between.
>
> The Ice was here, the Ice was there,
>   The Ice was all around:
> It crack<e>d and growl<e>d, and roar<e>d and howl<e>d(—)<,>
>   A wild and ceaseless sound.   60

1817

> And through the drifts the snowy clift/s/   The land of   55
> Did send a dismal sheen: ice, and of
> Nor shapes of men nor beasts we ken —   fearful
> The ice was all between.   sounds, where
>   no living
>   thing was to
>   be seen.
> The ice was here, the ice was there,
> The ice was all around: 60
> It cracked and growled, and roar/e/d and howl/e/d,
> Like noises in a swound!

1798

> At length did cross an Albatross,
>   Thorough the Fog it came;
> And an it were a Christian Soul,
>   We hail'd it in God's name.
>
> The Marineres gave it biscuit-worms,   65
>   And round and round it flew:
> The Ice did split with a Thunder-fit;
>   The Helmsman steer'd us thro'.

1800

> At length did cross an Albatross,
>   Thorough the Fog it came;
> As if it had been a Christian Soul,
>   We hail<e>d it in God's name.
>
> The Mariners gave it biscuit-worms,   65
>   And round and round it flew:
> The Ice did split with a Thunder-fit;
>   The Helmsman steer<e>d us thro<ugh>.

1817

Till a great
sea-bird,
called the
Albatross,
came through
the snow-fog,
and was
received with
great joy and
hospitality.

> At length did cross an Albatross:
> Thorough the fog it came;
> As if it had been a Christian soul,   65
> We hailed it in God's name.
>
> It ate the food it ne'er had eat,[13]
> And round and round it flew.
> The ice did split with a thunder-fit;
> The helmsman steer/e/d us through!   70

---

[13] Coleridge emends from "ate," *YSL*.

1798

And a good south wind sprung up behind,
  The Albatross did follow;   70
And every day for food or play
  Came to the Marinere's hollo!

In mist or cloud on mast or shroud
  It perch'd for vespers nine,
Whiles all the night thro' fog smoke-white,[14]   75
  Glimmer'd the white moon-shine.

1800

And a good South wind sprung up behind.[,]
  The Albatross did follow;   70
And every day for food or play
  Came to the Mariner's hollo!

In mist or cloud on mast or shroud
  It perch<e>d for vespers nine,
Whiles all the night thro<ugh> fog-smoke white   75
  Glimmer<e>d the white moon-shine.<">

1817

And a good south wind sprung up behind;
The Albatross did follow,
And every day, for food or play,
Came to the |M|ariner|'|s/'/ hollo!

In mist or cloud, on mast or shroud,   75
It perch[e]d for vespers nine;
Whiles all the night, through fog-smoke white,
Glimmered the white Moon-shine.

And lo! the
Albatross
proveth a bird
of good omen,
and followeth
the ship as it
returned
northward,
through fog
and floating
ice.

---

[14] "For 'fog smoke-white,' read 'fog-smoke white'" (Errata, *LB*). In the copy of the Bristol issue (#2604) in the Wren Library, Trinity College, Cambridge, the improper hyphen has been rubbed out and the correct hyphen inked in.

1798

> "God save thee, ancyent Marinere!
>   "From the fiends that plague thee thus —
> "Why look'st thou so?" — with my cross bow
>   I shot the Albatross.   80

1800

> "God save thee, ancient[15] Mariner!
>   (")From the fiends that plague thee thus<!> —
> (")Why look'st thou so?" — <">With my cross bow
>   I shot the Albatross.<">   80

1817

The ancient
Mariner
inhospitably
killeth the
pious bird of
good omen.

> "God save thee, ancient Mariner!
> From the fiends, that plague thee thus|!|/ — /
> Why look'st thou so?" — With my cross-bow
> I shot the ALBATROSS!   80

---

[15] 1805 prints "antient."

1798

II.[16]

The Sun came up upon the right,
  Out of the Sea came he;
And broad as a weft upon the left
  Went down into the Sea.

1800

II.

<">The Sun now rose upon the right,[17]
  Out of the Sea came he;
Still hid in mist; and on the left
  Went down into the Sea.

1817

THE RIME OF THE ANCIENT MARINER.
PART THE SECOND.

THE Sun now rose upon the right:
Out of the sea came he,
Still hid in mist, and on the left
Went down into the sea.

85

---

[16] In all editions each new part begins a new page.
[17] "Left" appears as a cancelled word in the line above (Griggs I:599).

1798

And the good south wind still blew behind,   85
  But no sweet Bird did follow
Ne any day for food or play
  Came to the Marinere's hollo!

And I had done an hellish thing
  And it would work 'em woe: 90
For all averr'd, I had kill'd the Bird
  That made the Breeze to blow.

1800

And the good <S>outh wind still blew behind,   85
  But no sweet Bird did follow,
Nor any day for food or play
Came to the Mariner's hollo!

And I had done an hellish thing<,>
  And it would work ['em]¹⁸ woe: 90
For all averr<e>d, I had kill<e>d the Bird
  That made the Breeze to blow.

1817

And the good south wind still blew behind,
But no sweet bird did follow,
Nor any day for food or play
Came to the mariners' hollo!   90

His ship-
mates cry out   And I had done an hellish thing, ·
against the   And it would work 'em woe:
ancient Mari-   For all averred, I had killed the bird
ner, for killing   That made the breeze to blow.
the bird of   Ah wretch! said they, the bird to slay,   95
good luck.   That made the breeze to blow!

---

¹⁸ 1800 prints "e'm."

1798

Ne dim ne red, like God's own head,
  The glorious Sun uprist:
Then all averr'd, I had kill'd the Bird   95
  That brought the fog and mist.
'Twas right, said they, such birds to slay
  That bring the fog and mist.

1800

Nor dim nor red, like an Angel's head,
  The glorious Sun uprist:
Then all averr<e>d, I had kill<e>d the Bird   95
  That brought the fog and mist.
'Twas right, said they, such birds to slay
  That bring the fog and mist.

1817

Nor dim nor red, like God's own head,
The glorious Sun uprist:
Then all averred, I had killed the bird
That brought the fog and mist.
'Twas right, said they, such birds to slay,
That bring the fog and mist.

But when the
fog cleared
off, they jus-
tify the same,
and thus   100
make them-
selves accom-
plices in the
crime.

1798

> The breezes blew, the white foam flew,
>   The furrow follow'd free: 100
> We were the first that ever burst
>   Into that silent Sea.
>
> Down dropt the breeze, the Sails dropt down,
>   'Twas sad as sad could be
> And we did speak only to break   105
>   The silence of the Sea.

1800

> The breezes blew, the white foam flew,
>   The furrow follow\<e\>d free: 100
> We were the first that ever burst
>   Into that silent \<S\>ea.
>
> Down dropt the breeze, the Sails dropt down,
>   'Twas sad as sad could be,
> And we did speak only to break   105
>   The silence of the Sea.

1817

The fair breeze continues; the ship enters the Pacific Ocean and sails northward, even till it reaches the Line.

The ship hath been suddenly becalmed.

> The fair breeze blew, the white foam flew,
> The furrow stream'd off free:[19]
> We were the first that ever burst   105
> Into that silent sea.
>
> Down dropt the breeze, the sails dropt down,
> 'Twas sad as sad could be;
> And we did speak only to break
> The silence of the sea!   110

---

[19] In the former edition the line was,
        The furrow follow'd free:
but I had not been long on board a ship, before I perceived that this was the image as seen by a spectator from the shore, or from another vessel. From the ship itself the *Wake* appears like a brook flowing off from the stern. (Coleridge's note in *SL*). 1828 prints, "The furrow followed free."

1798

All in a hot and copper sky
  The bloody sun at noon,
Right up above the mast did stand,
  No bigger than the moon.   110

Day after day, day after day,
  We stuck, ne breath ne motion,
As idle as a painted Ship
  Upon a painted Ocean.

1800

All in a hot and copper sky
  The bloody sun at noon,
Right up above the mast did stand,
  No bigger than the moon.   110

Day after day, day after day,
  We stuck, nor breath nor motion,
As idle as a painted Ship
  Upon a painted Ocean.

1817

All in a hot and copper sky,
The bloody Sun, at noon,
Right up above the mast did stand,
No bigger than the Moon.

Day after day, day after day,   115
We stuck, nor breath nor motion,
As idle as a painted ship
Upon a painted ocean.

1798

Water, water, every where[20]   115
  And all the boards did shrink;
Water, water, every where,
  Ne any drop to drink.

The very deeps did rot: O Christ!
  That ever this should be!   120
Yea, slimy things did crawl with legs
  Upon the slimy Sea.

1800

Water, water, every where,   115
  And all the boards did shrink;
Water, water, every where,
  Nor any drop to drink.

The very deeps did rot: O Christ!
  That ever this should be!   120
Yea, slimy things did crawl with legs
  Upon the slimy Sea.

1817

And the   Water, water, every where,
Albatross   And all the boards did shrink;   120
begins to be   Water water, every where,
avenged.   Nor any drop to drink.

                           The very deep did rot: O Christ!
                           That ever this should be!
                           Yea, slimy things did crawl with legs 125
                           Upon the slimy sea.

---

[20] The Wren Library's copy of the Arch issue of *LB* (#2604) has a comma at the end of this
line, though it has probably been inked in.

1798

    About, about, in reel and rout
      The Death-fires danc'd at night;
    The water, like a witch's oils,   125
      Burnt green and blue and white.

    And some in dreams assured were
      Of the Spirit that plagued us so:
    Nine fathom deep he had follow'd us   130
      From the Land of Mist and Snow.

1800

    About, about, in reel and rout
      The Death-fires danc<e>d at night;
    The water, like a witch's oils,   125
      Burnt green and blue and white.

    And some in dreams assured were
      Of the Spirit that plagued us so:
    Nine fathom deep he had follow<e>d us
      From the Land of Mist and Snow.   130

1817

    About, about, in reel and rout
    The death-fires danced at night;
    The water, like a witch's oils,
    Burnt green, and blue and white.   130

    And some in dreams assured were
    Of the spirit that plagued us so:
    Nine fathom deep he had followed us
    From the land of mist and snow.

> A spirit had followed them; one of the invisible inhabitants of this planet, neither departed souls nor angels; concerning whom the

1798

And every tongue thro' utter drouth
  Was wither'd at the root;
We could not speak no more than if
  We had been choked with soot.

Ah wel-a-day! what evil looks   135
  Had I from old and young;
Instead of the Cross the Albatross
  About my neck was hung.

1800

And every tongue thro<ugh> utter drouth
  Was withered at the root;
We could not speak no more than if
  We had been choked with soot.

Ah well-a-day! what evil looks   135
  Had I from old and young(;)<!>
Instead of the Cross the Albatross
  About my neck was hung.

1817

learned Jew,
Josephus, and
the Platonic   And every tongue, through utter drought,[21]   135
Constantino-   Was wither/e/d at the root;
politan, Mi-   We could not speak, no more than if
chael Psellus,   We had been choak'd with soot.
may be
consulted. They are very numerous, and there is no
climate or element without one or more.

The Ship-
mates, in
their sore
distress,   Ah! well a-day! <W>hat evil looks
would fain   Had I from old and young!   140
throw the   Instead of the cross, the Albatross
whole guilt   About my neck was hung.
on the ancient
mariner: in sign whereof they hang the
dead sea-bird round his neck.

---

[21] *YSL* prints "drouth," and in the margin Coleridge changes this to "drought." 1828 prints
"drought."

1798

III.

I saw a something in the Sky
  No bigger than my fist;   140
At first it seem'd a little speck
  And then it seem'd a mist:
It mov'd and mov'd, and took at last
  A certain shape, I wist.

1800

III.

<">So pas(t)<s'd>²² a weary {T}ime; each {T}hroat
  Was parch<e>d, and glaz<e>d each eye,
When, looking westward, I beheld   140
  A something in the {S}ky.

1817

THE RIME OF THE ANCIENT MARINER.
PART THE THIRD.

THERE passed a weary time. Each throat
Was parched, and glazed each eye.
A weary time! a weary time!
How glazed each weary eye!   145
When looking westward, I beheld   The ancient
A something in the sky.   Mariner be-
                                           holdeth a sign
                                           in the ele-
                                           ment afar off.

---

²²Coleridge's instruction reads "pass'd" (Griggs I:599). The printed texts of 1800 and 1802 read "past"; "pass'd" appears in 1805.

1798

A speck, a mist, a shape, I wist!   145
  And still it ner'd and ner'd;
And, an it dodg'd a water-sprite,
  It plung'd and tack'd and veer'd.

1800

At first it seem<e>d a little speck,[23]
  And then it seemed a mist\;\[:]
It mov<e>d and mov<e>d, and took at last\,\
  A certain shape, I wist.   145

A speck, a mist, a shape, I wist!
  And still it ner'd and ner'd;
And(,) as if it dodg<e>d a water-sprite,
  It plung<e>d and tack<e>d and veer<e>d.

1817

At first it seem/e/d a little speck,
And then it seem/e/d a mist: 150
It moved and moved, and took at last
A certain shape, I wist.

A speck, a mist, a shape, I wist!
And still it near/e/d and near/e/d:[24]
|And,| /A/s if it dodged a water-sprite,   155
It plunged and tack/e/d and veer/e/d.

---

[23] No comma in 1802.
[24] Coleridge tried three different revisions in *YSL*, one marked through completely (possibly
"'rs 'rs"?), another marked through but legible as "near." In the opposite margin appears the simple
revision, "a/ a/."

1798

With throat unslack'd, with black lips bak'd
  Ne could we laugh, ne wail: 150
Then while thro' drouth all dumb they stood
I bit my arm and suck'd the blood
  And cry'd, A sail! a sail!

With throat unslack'd, with black lips bak'd
  Agape they hear'd me call: 155
Gramercy! they for joy did grin
And all at once their breath drew in
  As they were drinking all.

1800

With throat unslack<e>d, with black lips bak<e>d   150
  We could nor laugh nor wail;
Thro<ugh> utter {D}routh all dumb we stood
Till I bit my arm and suck<e>d the blood,
  And cry'd,[25] A sail! a sail!

With throat unslack<e>d, with black lips bak<e>d
  Agape they heard me call: 155
Gramercy! they for joy did grin<,>
And all at once their breath drew in
  As they were drinking all.

1817

With throat unslack/e/d, with black lips baked,   At its nearer
We could nor laugh nor wail;   approach, it
Through utter drought all dumb we stood!   seemeth him
                                     to be a ship;
I bit my arm, I sucked the blood,   and at a dear
And cried, A sail! a sail!   ransom he   160
                                     freeth his
                                   speech from
With throat unslacked, with black lips baked,   the bonds of
Agape they heard me call: thirst.
Gramercy! they for joy did grin,   A flash of joy.
And all at once their breath drew in,
  As they were drinking all.   165

---

[25] 1805 prints "cried."

1798

> She doth not tack from side to side —
>   Hither to work us weal   160
> Withouten wind, withouten tide
>   She steddies with upright keel.

1800

> {'}See! See!{"} (I cry'd[26]) {'}she tacks no more!   160
>   {'}Hither to work us {W}eal\;\
> {'}Without a breeze, without a {T}ide
>   {'}She steddies with upright {K}eel![27]

1817

And horror   See! see! (I cried) she tacks no more!
follows. For   Hither to work us weal;
can it be a   Without a breeze, without a tide,
ship[28] that   She steddies[29] with upright keel!   170
comes onward
without wind
or tide?

---

[26] 1805 prints "cried." Parenthesis in text.

[27] Coleridge's instuctions in the letter to Biggs and Cottle (Griggs I:599) read as follows:
"p. 16. Last line but one instead of
       'Withouten wind, withouten tide'
print 'without or wind or current tide['] —
in the same stanza instead of 'She doth not tack from side' print

       'See! see' (I cry'd) she tacks no more![']'"

Griggs notes these instructions are crossed out; Coleridge then instructs the stanza to be printed as above.
(Square brackets are in Griggs' text.)

[28] 1828 prints "ship" without emphasis.

[29] 1828 prints "steadies."

1798

The western wave was all a flame,
  The day was well nigh done!
Almost upon the western wave   165
  Rested the broad bright Sun;
When that strange shape drove suddenly
  Betwixt us and the Sun.

And strait the Sun was fleck'd with bars
  (Heaven's mother send us grace)   170
As if thro' a dungeon grate he peer'd
  With broad and burning face.

1800

The western wave was all a flame(,)<.>
  The day was well nigh done!   165
Almost upon the western wave
  Rested the broad bright Sun;
When that strange shape drove suddenly
  Betwixt us and the Sun.

And strai<gh>t the Sun was fleck<e>d with bars
  (Heaven's Mother send us grace<!>)   170
As if thro<ugh> a dungeon grate he peer<e>d
  With broad and burning face.

1817

The western wave was all a-flame.
The day was well nigh done!
Almost upon the western wave
Rested the broad bright Sun;
When that strange shape drove suddenly   175
Betwixt us and the Sun.

And straight the Sun was flecked with bars,   It seemeth
(Heaven's Mother send us grace!)   him but the
As if through a dungeon-grate he peer/e/d,   skeleton of a
With broad and burning face.   ship.
                                 180

1798

> Alas! (thought I, and my heart beat loud)
>   How fast she neres and neres!
> Are those *her* Sails that glance in the Sun   175
>   Like restless gossameres?

1800

> Alas!(thought I, and my heart beat loud)
>   How fast she neres and neres!   175
> Are those *her* Sails that glance in the Sun
>   Like restless gossameres?

1817

> Alas! (thought I, and my heart beat loud)
> How fast she nears and nears![30]
> Are those *her* sails that glance in the Sun,
> Like restless gossameres|?|/!/

---

[30] *YSL* prints "neres," but Coleridge comments in the margin, "Perhaps 'nears' would be better: as I have not elsewhere kept the old spelling."

1798

> Are those *her* naked ribs, which fleck'd
> The sun that did behind them peer?
> And are those two all, all the crew,
> That woman and her fleshless Pheere?   180

> > Are those her ribs, which fleck'd the Sun,
> > Like the bars of a dungeon grate?
> > And are these two all, all the crew
> > That woman and her Mate?[31]

> > This Ship, it was a plankless Thing,   185
> > A rare Anatomy!
> > A plankless Spectre — and it mov'd
> > Like a Being of the Sea!
> > The Woman and a fleshless Man
> > Therein sate merrily.[32]   190

1800

> Are those *her* Ribs, thro<ugh> which the Sun
> Did peer, as thro<ugh> a grate?
> And are those two all, all her crew,
> That Woman, and her Mate?   180

1817

> Are those *her* ribs through which the Sun
> Did peer, as through a grate?
> And is that Woman all her crew?
> Is that a DEATH? and are there two?
> Is DEATH that woman's mate?

And its ribs are seen as bars on the face of the setting Sun. The spectre-woman and her death-mate, and no other on board the skeleton-ship.   185

---

[31] Coleridge's addition on page 18 in the Bristol *LB* (#2603).
[32] Coleridge's addition at the bottom of page 18 in the Bristol *LB* (#2603). Preceeding the variant is the instruction, in his hand, "Insert the following stanza — ."

1798

>
> *His* bones were black with many a crack,
>   All black and bare, I ween;
> Jet-black and bare, save where with rust
> Of mouldy damps and charnel crust
>   They're patch'd with purple and green.   195
>
> *Her* lips are red, *her* looks are free,
>   *Her* locks are yellow as gold:
> Her skin is as white as leprosy,
> And she is far liker Death than he;
>   Her flesh makes the still air cold.   200

1800

>
> *His* bones were black with many a crack,
>   All black and bare, I ween;
> Jet-black and bare, save where with rust
> Of mouldy damps and charnel crust   185
>   They were patch<e>d with purple and green.
>
> *Her* lips were red, *her* looks were free,
>   *Her* locks were yellow as gold:
> Her skin was as white as leprosy,
> And she was far liker Death than he;   190
>   Her flesh made the still air cold.

1817

> Like vessel, *Her* lips were red, *her* looks were free,   190
> like crew!   Her locks were yellow as gold:
>   Her skin was as white as leprosy,
>   The Night-Mair[33] LIFE-IN-DEATH was she,
>   Who thicks man's blood with cold.

---

[33] "In James Gillman's copy, now in the Norton Perkins collection Harvard, Coleridge himself . . . has deleted the 'i' in 'mair' and added a final 'e'" (Lowes 527n). 1828 prints "mare."

1798

> The naked Hulk alongside came
>   And the Twain were playing dice;
> "The Game is done! I've won, I've won!"
>   Quoth she, and whistled thrice.
>
> A gust of wind sterte up behind   205
>   And whistled thro' his bones;
> Thro' the holes of his eyes and the hole of his mouth
>   Half-whistles and half-groans.

1800

> The naked Hulk alongside came
>   And the Twain were playing dice;
> "The Game is done! I've won, I've won!"   195
>   Quoth she, and whistled thrice.
>
> A gust of wind sterte up behind
>   And whistled thro<ugh> his bones;
> Thro' the holes[34] of his eyes and the hole of his mouth
>   Half-whistles and half-groans.

1817

> The naked hulk alongside came,   DEATH, and   195
> And the twain were casting dice;   LIFE-IN-
> "The game is done, I've,[35] I've won" DEATH have
> Quoth she, and whistles thrice.   diced for the
>   ship's crew,
>   and she (the
>   latter) win-
> A gust of wind sterte up behind   neth the an-
> And whistled through his bones;   cient Mariner.
> Through the holes of his eyes and the hole of his mouth,   200
> Half whistles and half groans.[36]

---

[34] 1802 and 1805 read "hole."
[35] As in both 1817 and 1828.
[36] "Upon this Coleridge comments as follows in the copy of 'Sibylline Leaves' in the possession of Mr. Stuart Montagu Samuel: 'This stanza I had earnestly urged the printer to omit, but he was a coxcomb, and had an opinion of his own, forsooth! The Devil daub him! (*i.e.* his own Devil)'" (Garnett 285). Also see Lowes 533n, quoting Coleridge: "This stanza was struck out by the Author, and reprinted either by the Oversight or the Self-opinion of the Printer to whom the Author was indebted for various intended improvements of his Poems. S.T. Coleridge." The stanza is absent from 1828.

1798

With never a whisper in the Sea[37]
  Oft[38] darts the Spectre-ship;   210
While clombe above the Eastern bar
The horned Moon,[39] with one bright Star
  Almost atween the tips.

One after one by the horned Moon
  (Listen, O Stranger! to me)   215
Each turn'd his face with a ghastly pang
  And curs'd me with his ee.

---

[37] Hutchinson prints a semi-colon at the end of this line (as in 1800).

[38] As in the Bristol *LB* (#2603). A misprint; corrected in ink to"Off" in all but three extant copies. See Hutchinson lx. See Griggs I:600: "P. 19. Line 10 For 'Oft' print 'Off'."

[39] It is a common superstition among sailors "that something is about to happen whenever a star dogs the moon" (Note by Coleridge on the bottom of page 19 of the Bristol *LB* [#2603], though not printed until the edition of 1877-80. Campbell comments: "But no sailor ever saw a star within the nether tip of a horned moon" (598). But compare Lowes' discussion of "two remarkable sets of observations, communicated...each with the barely less than sensational heading: 'An Account of an Appearance of Light, like a Star, seen in the dark Part of the Moon, on Friday the 7th of March, 1794'" (166). And see Hutchinson, who quotes the 26 January 1732 entry of Captain Thomas James' Journal: "I observed, when the eastern edge of the moon did touch the planet Mars, the Lion's-Heart was then in the east quarter 21.45. above the horizon" (Hutchinson 216n).

1800

With never a whisper in the Sea   200
  Off darts thc Spectre-ship;
Whilc clombe above the Eastern bar
The horned Moon, with one bright Star
  Almost between the tips.

With never a whisper on the main   205
  Off shot the spectre-ship;
And stifled words & groans of pain
                        murmuring
    Mix'd on each ~~trembling~~ lip/
And/ we look'd round, & we look'd up,
    And fear at our hearts, as at a cup,   210
      The Life-blood seem'd to sip
The Sky was dull, & dark the night,
The Helmsman's Face by his lamp gleam'd bright,
    From the sails the Dews did drip/
          clombe
Till ~~rose~~ above the Eastern Bar
The horned moon, with one bright Star   215
Within its nether Tip.[40]

One after one by the horned Moon
(Listen, O Stranger! to me)[41]
Each turn<e>d his face with a ghastly pang
And curs<e>d me with his ee.   220

---

[40] Between 1806 and 1811; Add MS 47508 f. 5, in the British Library. Printed in *CN* II:2880 and note, in EHC I:195, and in Campbell 598. Campbell is unsure of the date, stating that the passage comes from some papers "dated from 1806, 1807, and 1810."

[41] Parenthesis in text.

1817

Within the tropics there is no Twilight. As
the sun sinks, the Evening Gun is fired,
and the Starry Heaven is at once overall,
like men in ambush that have been
listening for the signal — [...?]
blare!=(Row)[?][42]

The Sun's rim dips; the stars rush out:
At one stride comes the dark;
With far-heard whisper, o'er the sea,   205
Off shot the spectre-bark.

Within the Tropics there is no Twilight. At the moment,
the second, that the Sun sinks, the Stars appear all at
once as if at the word of a command announced by the
evening Gun, in our W. India Islands.[43]

Between the Tropics there is no twilight.
As the Sun's last segment dips down and
the evening gun is fired the
constellations appear arrayed.[44]

No twilight where there is no latitude nor
yet on either side within the Park and
Race-course of the Sun. — [45]

No twilight within the
courts of the sun.[46]

We listen/e/d and look/e/d sideways up!
Fear at my heart, as at a cup,
My life-blood seemed to sip!
The stars were dim, and thick the night,   210
The steersman's face by his lamp gleamed white;

At the rising
of the Moon,

From the sails the dews did drip —
Till clombe above the eastern bar
The horned Moon, with one bright star
Within the nether tip.   215

One after
another,

One after one, by the star-dogged Moon,
Too quick for groan or sigh/t/,
Each turned his face with a ghastly pang,
And curs/e/d me with his eye.

---

[42] This version written in the Stanford copy of *SL*. This copy is described in Johnson, 456-58. Brackets in her text.

[43] This version of the gloss appears in a copy of *SL* at Harvard. Inscribed, "Highgate, 29 July 1820."

[44] See Garnett 286. This version appears as an annotation "in Mr. Samuel's copy of *Sibylline Leaves* (not the same as that seen by Mr. Dykes Campbell)."

[45] This version written in a copy of *SL* at Harvard. See Lowes 152-53.

[46] This version of the gloss appears first in 1828.

1798

    Four times fifty living men,
      With never a sigh or groan,
    With heavy thump, a lifeless lump   220
     They dropp'd down one by one.

    Their souls did from their bodies fly, —
      They fled to bliss or woe;
    And every soul it pass'd me by,
     Like the whiz of my Cross-bow.   225

1800

    Four times fifty living men,
      With never a sigh or groan,
    With heavy thump, a lifeless lump
     They dropp<e>d down one by one.   225

    Their souls did from their bodies fly, —
      They fled to bliss or woe;
    And every soul it pass<e>d me by,
     Like the whiz of my Cross-bow.<">

1817

    Four times fifty living men,   His ship-   220
    (And I heard nor sigh nor groan) mates drop
    With heavy thump, a lifeless lump, down dead;
    They dropped down one by one.

    The souls did from their bodies fly, — But LIFE-IN-
    They fled to bliss or woe!   DEATH be-
    And every soul, it passed me by, gins her work 225
    Like the whiz of my CROSS-BOW! on the ancient
                                 Mariner.

1798

IV.

"I fear thee, ancyent Marinere!
  "I fear thy skinny hand;
"And thou art long and lank and brown
  "As is the ribb'd Sea-sand.

"I fear thee and thy glittering eye   230
  "And thy skinny hand so brown —
Fear not, fear not, thou wedding guest!
  This body dropt not down.

1800

IV.

"I fear thee, ancient Mariner!   230
  (")I fear thy skinny hand;
(")And thou art long and lank and brown\,\
  (")As is the ribb<e>d Sea-sand.

(")I fear thee and thy glittering eye
  (")And thy skinny hand so brown<">—   235
<">Fear not, fear not, thou wedding guest!
  This body dropt not down.

1817

THE RIME OF THE ANCIENT MARINER.
PART THE FOURTH.

The wedding-
guest feareth
that a spirit is
talking to him;

"I FEAR thee, ancient Mariner!
I fear thy skinny hand!
And thou art long, and lank, and brown,   230
As is the ribbed sea-sand.[47]

But the an-
cient Mariner
assureth him
of his bodily
life, and pro-

I fear thee and thy glittering eye,
And thy skinny hand, so brown." —
Fear not, fear not, thou Wedding-Guest!
This body dropt not down.   235

---

[47] For the last two lines of this stanza, I am indebted to Mr. WORDSWORTH. It was on a delightful walk from Nether Stowey to Dulverton, with him and his sister, in the Autumn of 1797, that this Poem was planned, and in part composed. (Coleridge's note, *SL*.)

1798

   Alone, alone, all all alone
    Alone on the wide wide Sea;   235
   And Christ would take no pity on
    My soul in agony.

   The many men so beautiful,
    And they all dead did lie!
   And a million million slimy things   240
    Liv'd on — and so did I.

1800

   Alone, alone, all all alone,
    Alone on the wide wide Sea;
   And Christ would take no pity on   240
    My soul in agony.

   The many men so beautiful,
    And they all dead did lie!
   And a million million slimy things
    Liv<e>d on — and so did I.   245

1817

   Alone, alone, all, all alone,   ceedeth to
   Alone on a wide wide sea!   relate his hor-
   And never a saint took pity on   rible penance.
   My soul in agony.

   The many men, so beautiful!   He despiseth   240
   And they all dead did lie: the creatures
   And a thousand thousand slimy things of the calm,
   Liv/e/d on; and so did I.

1798

> I look'd upon the rotting Sea,
>   And drew my eyes away;
> I look'd upon the eldritch deck,
>   And there the dead men lay.   245
>
> I look'd to Heaven, and try'd to pray;
>   But or ever a prayer had gusht,
> A wicked whisper came and made
>   My heart as dry as dust.

1800

> I look<e>d upon the rotting Sea
>   And drew my eyes away;
> I look<e>d upon the ghastly deck,
>   And there the dead men lay.
>
> I look<e>d to Heaven, and try'd[48] to pray;   250
>   But or ever a prayer had gusht,
> A wicked whisper came and made
>   My heart as dry as dust.

1817

And envieth
that *they*[49]
should live,
and so many
lie dead.

> I look/e/d upon the rotting sea,
> And drew my eyes away;   245
> I look'd upon the rotting deck,
> And there the dead men lay.
>
> I looked to Heaven, and tried to pray;
> But or ever a prayer had gusht,
> A wicked whisper came, and made   250
> My heart as dry as dust.

---

[48] 1805 prints "tried."
[49] 1828 prints no emphasis.

1798

I clos'd my lids and kept them close,   250
  Till the balls like pulses beat;
For the sky and the sea, and the sea and the sky
Lay like a load on my weary eye,
  And the dead were at my feet.

The cold sweat melted from their limbs,   255
  Ne rot, ne reek did they;
The look with which they look'd on me,
  Had never pass'd away.

1800

I clos<e>d my lids and kept them close,
  Till the balls like pulses beat;   255
For the sky and the sea, and the sea and the sky
Lay like a load on my weary eye,
  And the dead were at my feet.

The cold sweat melted from their limbs,
  Nor rot(,) nor reek did they;   260
The look with which they look<e>d on me,
  Had never pass<e>d away.

1817

I closed my lids, and kept them close,
And the balls like pulses beat;
For the sky and the sea, and the sea and the sky
Lay, like a cloud,[50] on my weary eye,   255
And the dead were at my feet.

The cold sweat melted from their limbs,   *But the curse*
Nor rot nor reek did they: *liveth for him*
The look with which they look/e/d on me   *in the eye of*
Had never pass/e/d away.   *the dead men.*   260

---

[50] Errata 1817 reads, "For cloud read load." 1828 prints "load."

1798

An orphan's curse would drag to Hell
  A spirit from on high: 260
But O! more horrible than that
  Is the curse in a dead man's eye!
Seven days, seven nights I saw that curse,
  And yet I could not die.

1800

An orphan's curse would drag to Hell
  A spirit from on high:
But O! more horrible than that   265
  Is the curse in a dead man's eye!
Seven days, seven nights I saw that curse,
  And yet I could not die.

1817

An orphan's curse would drag to Hell
A spirit from on high;
But oh! more horrible than that
Is the curse in a dead man's eye!
Seven days, seven nights, I saw that curse,
And yet I could not die.   265

1798

The moving Moon went up the sky   265
  And no where did abide:
Softly she was going up
  And a star or two beside —

Her beams bemock'd the sultry main
  Like morning frosts yspread;   270
But where the ship's huge shadow lay,
The charmed water burnt alway
  A still and awful red.

1800

The moving Moon went up the sky\,\   270
  And no where did abide:
Softly she was going up
  And a star or two beside —

Her beams bemock<e>d the sultry main
  Like April hoar-frost spread;[51]
But where the [S]hip's huge shadow lay,   275
The charmed water burnt alway
  A still and awful red.

1817

The moving Moon went up the sky,
And no where did abide:
Softly she was going up,
And a star or two beside —   270

Her beams bemock/e/d the sultry main,
Like April hoar-frost spread;
But where the ship's huge shadow lay,
The charmed water burnt alway
A still and awful red.   275

In his loneliness and fixedness|,| he yearneth towards the journeying Moon and the stars that still sojourn, yet still move onward; and every where the blue sky|,| belongs to them, and is their appointed rest, and their native country|,| and their own natural homes which they enter unannounced as lords that are certainly expected|,| and yet there is a silent joy at their arrival.

---

[51] Griggs I:600.

1798

Beyond the shadow of the ship   275
  I watch'd the water-snakes:
They mov'd in tracks of shining white;
And when they rear'd, the elfish light
  Fell off in hoary flakes.

Within the shadow of the ship
  I watch'd their rich attire: 280
Blue, glossy green, and velvet black
They coil'd and swam; and every track
  Was a flash of golden fire.

───

1800

Beyond the shadow of the ship
  I watch<e>d the water-snakes: 280
They mov<e>d in tracks of shining white;
And when they rear<e>d, the elfish light
  Fell off in hoary flakes.

Within the shadow of the ship
  I watch<e>d their rich attire:
Blue, glossy green, and velvet black   285
They coil<e>d and swam; and every track
  Was a flash of golden fire.

───

1817

By the light
of the Moon he
beholdeth
God's crea-
tures of the
great calm.

Beyond the shadow of the ship,
  I watch/e/d the water-snakes:
They moved in tracks of shining white,
And when they reared, the elfish light
  Fell off in hoary flakes.   280

Within the shadow of the ship
  I watch/e/d their rich attire:
Blue, glossy green, and velvet black,
They coiled and swam; and every track
  Was a flash of golden fire.   285

1798

    O happy living things! no tongue
      Their beauty might declare:
    A spring of love gusht from my heart,   285
      And I bless'd them unaware!
    Sure my kind saint took pity on me,
      And I bless'd them unaware.

    The self-same moment I could pray;   290
      And from my neck so free
    The Albatross fell off, and sank
      Like lead into the sea.

1800

    O happy living things! no tongue
      Their beauty might declare:
    A spring of love gusht from my heart,   290
      And I bless<e>d them unaware!
    Sure my kind saint took pity on me,
      And I bless<e>d them unaware.

    The self-same moment I could pray;
      And from my neck so free   295
    The Albatross fell off, and sank
      Like lead into the sea.

1817

    O happy living things! no tongue   Their beauty
    Their beauty might declare: and their
    A spring of love gusht from my heart,   happiness.
    And I blessed them unaware|!|/?/
    Sure my kind saint took pity on me,   He blesseth
    And I blessed them unaware.   them in his   290
      heart.

    The self same moment I could pray;   The spell
    And from my neck so free   begins to
    The Albatross fell off, and sank   break.
    Like lead into the sea.   295

1798

V.

O sleep, it is a gentle thing
  Belov'd from pole to pole!
To Mary-queen the praise be yeven
She sent the gentle sleep from heaven
  That slid into my soul.

295

1800

V.

<">O sleep, it is a gentle thing
  Belov<e>d from pole to pole!
To Mary-queen the praise be given<,>
She sent the gentle sleep from heaven
  That slid into my soul.

300

1817

THE RIME OF THE ANCIENT MARINER.
PART THE FIFTH.

O, SLEEP,[52] it is a gentle thing!
Belov/e/d from pole to pole!
To Mary Queen the praise be given|,|/!/
She sent the gentle sleep from Heaven,
That slid into my soul.

300

---

[52] 1828 prints "OH SLEEP!"

1798

The silly buckets on the deck
  That had so long remain'd,
I dreamt that they were fill'd with dew   300
  And when I awoke it rain'd.

My lips were wet, my throat was cold,
  My garments all were dank;
Sure I had drunken in my dreams
  And still my body drank.   305

1800

The silly buckets on the deck
  That had so long remain<e>d,
I dreamt that they were fill<e>d with dew<,>   305
  And when I awoke it rain<e>d.

My lips were wet, my throat was cold,
  My garments all were dank;
Sure I had drunken in my dreams<,>
  And still my body drank.   310

1817

The silly buckets on the deck,
That had so long remained,
I dreamt that they were filled with dew;
And when I awoke, it rained.

My lips were wet, my throat was cold,   305
My garments all were dank;
Sure I had drunken in my dreams,
And still my body drank.

By grace of
the holy
Mother, the
ancient Mari-
ner is refresh-
ed with rain.

1798

I mov'd and could not feel my limbs,
  I was so light, almost
I thought that I had died in sleep,
  And was a blessed Ghost.   310

The roaring wind! it roar'd far off,
  It did not come anear;
But with its sound it shook the sails
  That were so thin and sere.

1800

I mov<e>d and could not feel my limbs,
  I was so light, almost
I thought that I had died in sleep,
  And was a blessed Ghost.

And soon I heard a roaring wind\:\[,]   315
  It did not come anear;
But with its sound it shook the sails
  That were so thin and sere.

1817

He heareth
sounds, and
seeth
strange sights
and commo-
tions in the
sky and the
element.

I moved/,/ and could not feel my limbs|,|/:/
I was so light/,/ — almost   310
I thought that I had died in sleep,
And was a blessed ghost.

And soon I heard a roaring wind:
It did not come anear;
But with its sound it shook the sails/,/   315
That were so thin and sere.

1798

    The upper air bursts into life,   315
      And a hundred fire-flags sheen
    To and fro they are hurried about;
    And to and fro, and in and out
      The stars dance on between.

1800

    The upper air burst into life<,>
      And a hundred fire-flags sheen   320
    To and fro they were hurried about;
    And to and fro, and in and out
      The wan {S}tars danc<e>d between.

1817

    The upper air burst into life!
    And a hundred fire-flags sheen,
    To and fro they were hurried about|;|/!/
    And to and fro, and in and out,   320
    The wan stars danced between.

1798

The coming wind doth roar more loud;   320
  The sails do sigh, like sedge:
The rain pours down from one black cloud
  And the Moon is at its edge.

Hark! hark! the thick black cloud is cleft,
  And the Moon is at its side: 325
Like waters shot from some high crag,
The lightning falls with never a jag
  A river steep and wide.

1800

And the coming wind did roar more loud;
  And the sails did sigh like sedge: 325
And the rain pour<e>d down from one black cloud
  The moon was at its edge.

The thick black cloud was cleft, and still
  The Moon was at its side:
Like waters shot from some high crag,   330
The lightning fell with never a jag
  A river steep and wide.

1817

And the coming wind did roar more loud,
And the sails did sigh like sedge;
And the rain pour/e/d down from one black cloud;
The Moon was at its edge.   325

The thick black cloud was cleft, and still
The Moon was at its side:
Like waters shot from some high crag,
The lightning fell with never a jag,
A river steep and wide.   330

1798

The strong wind reach'd the ship: it roar'd
  And dropp'd down, like a stone!   330
Beneath the lightning and the moon
  The dead men gave a groan.

They groan'd, they stirr'd, they all uprose,
  Ne spake, ne mov'd their eyes:
It had been strange, even in a dream   335
  To have seen those dead men rise.

1800

The loud[53] wind never reach\<e\>d the Ship,
  Yet now the Ship mov\<e\>d on!
Beneath the lightning and the moon   335
  The dead men gave a groan.

They groan\<e\>d, they stirr\<e\>d, they all uprose,
  Nor spake, nor mov\<e\>d their eyes:
It had been strange, even in a dream
  To have seen those dead men rise.   340

1817

The loud wind never reached the ship,
Yet now the ship movcd on!
Beneath the lightning and the Moon,
The dead men gave a groan.

They groan/e/d, they stirr/e/d, they all uprose,   335
Nor spake, nor moved their eyes;
It had been strange, even in a dream,
To have seen those dead men rise.

The bodies of the ship's crew are inspirited,[54] and the ship moves on|.|/;/

---

[53] "Strong" appears as a cancelled word in the line above; see Griggs I:601.
[54] 1828 prints "inspired."

1798

> The helmsman steerd, the ship mov'd on;
>   Yet never a breeze up-blew;
> The Marineres all 'gan work the ropes,
>   Where they were wont to do:
> They rais'd their limbs like lifeless tools —   340
>   We were a ghastly crew.

1800

> The helmsman steerd,[55] the ship mov<e>d on;
>   Yet never a breeze up-blew;
> The Mariners all 'gan work the ropes,
>   Where they were wont to do:
> They rais<e>d their limbs like lifeless tools —   345
>   We were a ghastly crew.

1817

> The helmsman steered, the ship moved on;
> Yet never a breeze up blew;   340
> The mariners all 'gan work the ropes,
> Where they were wont to do:
> They raised their limbs like lifeless tools —
> We were a ghastly crew.

[55] 1802 prints "steer'd"; 1805 prints "steered."

1798

>The body of my brother's son
> Stood by me knee to knee:
>The body and I pull'd at one rope,
> But he said nought to me —   345
>And I quak'd to think of my own voice
> How frightful it would be!

1800

>The body of my brother's son
> Stood by me knee to knee:
>The body and I pull<e>d at one rope,
> But he said nought to me.<">

>"I fear thee, ancient Mariner!["]
> <">Be calm,[56] thou \W\edding<->\G\uest!
>'Twas not those[57] souls[,] that fled in pain,
> Which to their corses came again,
>But a troop of Spirits blest:

By the interception of 350
his kind saint a choir
of angels desc[ended]
from Heaven, &
entered into the dead
bod[ies] using the
bodies a[s] material
Instrum[ents].[58]

1817

>The body of my brother's son   345
>Stood by me, knee to knee:
>The body and I pulled at one rope,
>But he said nought to me.

>"I fear thee, ancient Mariner!"
>Be calm, thou Wedding-Guest!
>'Twas not those souls that fled in pain,
>Which to their corses came again,
>But a troop of spirits blest:

But not by
the souls of
the men, nor   350
by dæmons
of earth or
middle air,
but by a blessed

---

[56] "Fear not" appears as cancelled phrase in the line above; see Griggs I:601.
[57] "The" appears as cancelled word in the line above; see Griggs I:601.
[58] This gloss is cited by Bald, *TLS* 26 July 1934: 528.

1798

The day-light dawn'd — they dropp'd their arms,
    And cluster'd round the mast:
Sweet sounds rose slowly thro' their mouths   350
    And from their bodies pass'd.

Around, around, flew each sweet sound,
    Then darted to the sun:
Slowly the sounds came back again
    Now mix'd, now one by one.   355

1800

For when it dawn<e>d — they dropp<e>d their arms,   355
    And cluster<e>d round the mast:
Sweet sounds rose slowly thro<ugh> their mouths<,>
    And from their bodies pass<e>d.

Around, around, flew each sweet sound,
    Then darted to the sun: 360
Slowly the sounds came back again
    Now mix<e>d, now one by one.

1817

troop of an-   For when it dawned — they dropped their arms,
gelic spirits,   And clustered round the mast;   355
sent down by   Sweet sounds rose slowly through their mouths,
the invocation   And from their bodies passed.
of the guar-
dian saint.   Around, around, flew each sweet sound,
                       Then darted to the Sun/;/
                      Slowly the sounds came back again,   360
                       Now mixed, now one by one.

1798

    Sometimes a dropping from the sky
      I heard the Lavrock sing;
    Sometimes all little birds that are
    How they seem'd to fill the sea and air
      With their sweet jargoning.   360

    And now 'twas like all instruments,
      Now like a lonely flute;
    And now it is an angel's song
      That makes the heavens be mute.

1800

    Sometimes a<->dropping from the sky
      I heard the Sky-lark sing;
    Sometimes all little birds that are   365
    How they seem<e>d to fill the sea and air
      With their sweet jargoning(.)<!>

    And now 'twas like all instruments,
      Now like a lonely flute(;)<:>
    And now it is an angel's song   370
      That makes the heavens be mute.

1817

    Sometimes a-dropping from the sky[59]
    I heard the sky-lark sing;
    Sometimes all little birds that are,
    How they seemed to fill the sea and air   365
    With their sweet jargoning!

    And now 'twas like all instruments,
    Now like a lonely flute;
    And now it is an angel's song/,/
    That makes the Heavens be mute.   370

---

[59] Coleridge adds commas after the first word and at the end of the line, and then crosses out his instructions, *YSL*.

1798

> It ceas'd: yet still the sails made on   365
>   A pleasant noise till noon,
> A noise like of a hidden brook
>   In the leafy month of June,
> That to the sleeping woods all night
>   Singeth a quiet tune.   370

1800

> It ceas<e>d: yet still the sails made on
>   A pleasant noise till noon,
> A noise like of a hidden brook
>   In the leafy month of June,   375
> That to the sleeping woods all night
>   Singeth a quiet tune.

1817

> It ceased; yet still the sails made on
> A pleasant noise till noon,
> A noise like of a hidden brook
> In the leafy[60] month of June,
> That to the sleeping woods all night   375
> Singeth a quiet tune.

---

[60]*YSL* prints "pleasant," though crossed through.

1798

Listen, O listen, thou Wedding-guest!
   "Marinere! thou hast thy will:
"For that, which comes out of thine eye, doth make
   "My body and soul to be still."

Never sadder tale was told
   To a man of woman born: 375
Sadder and wiser thou wedding-guest!
   Thou'lt rise to-morrow morn.

Never sadder tale was heard
   By a man of woman born: 380
The Marineres all return'd to work
   As silent as beforne.

The Marineres all 'gan pull the ropes,
   But look at me they n'old:
Thought I, I am as thin as air--
   They cannot me behold.   385

1800

1817

1798

> Till noon we silently sail'd on
>   Yet never a breeze did breathe:
> Slowly and smoothly went the ship
>   Mov'd onward from beneath.   390
>
> Under the keel nine fathom deep
>   From the land of mist and snow
> The spirit slid: and it was He
>   That made the Ship to go.
> The sails at noon left off their tune   395
>   And the Ship stood still also.

1800

> Till noon we silently sail<e>d on<,>
>   Yet never a breeze did breathe:
> Slowly and smoothly went the Ship   380
>   Mov<e>d onward from beneath.
>
> Under the keel nine fathom deep
>   From the land of mist and snow
> The <S>pirit slid: and it was He
>   That made the Ship to go.   385
> The sails at noon left off their tune<,>
>   And the Ship stood still also.

1817

> Till noon we quietly sailed on,
> Yet never a breeze did breathe:
> Slowly and smoothly went the ship,
> Moved onward from beneath.   380

The lonesome spirit from the south-pole carries on the ship as far as the line, in obedience to the angelic troop|;|/,/ but still requireth vengeance.

> Under the keel nine fathom deep,
> From the land of mist and snow,
> The spirit slid|;| /:/ and it was he
> That made the ship to go.
> The sails at noon left off their tune,   385
> And the ship stood still also.

1798

The sun right up above the mast
  Had fix'd her to the ocean:
But in a minute she 'gan stir
  With a short uneasy motion —   400
Backwards and forwards half her length
  With a short uneasy motion.

Then, like a pawing horse let go,
  She made a sudden bound:
It flung the blood into my head,   405
  And I fell into a swound.

1800

The Sun right up above the mast
  Had fix<e>d her to the ocean:
But in a minute she 'gan stir   390
  With a short uneasy motion —
Backwards and forwards half her length<,>
  With a short uneasy motion.

Then, like a pawing horse let go,
  She made a sudden bound: 395
It flung the blood into my head,
  And I fell into a swound.

1817

The Sun, right up above the mast,[61]
Had fixt[62] her to the ocean;[63]
But in a minute she 'gan stir,
With a short uneasy motion —   390
Backwards and forwards half her length|,|
With a short uneasy motion.

Then like a pawing horse let go,
She made a sudden bound:
It flung the blood into my head,   395
And I fell down in a swound.

---

[61] The first comma of this line added *YSL*, the second comma crossed through with instruction also crossed through, and Stet(?) written in.
[62] 1828 prints "fixed."
[63] Colon replaced with semi-colon, *YSL*.

1798

How long in that same fit I lay,
  I have not to declare;
But ere my living life return'd,
I heard and in my soul discern'd   410
  Two voices in the air,

"Is it he? quoth one, "Is this the man?
  "By him who died on cross,
"With his cruel bow he lay'd full low
  "The harmless Albatross.   415

1800

How long in that same fit I lay,
  I have not to declare;
But ere my living life return<e>d,   400
I heard and in my soul discern<e>d
  Two voices in the air.

(")<'>Is it he?(")<'>[64] quoth one, (")<'>Is this the man?
  (")By him who died on cross,
(")With his cruel bow he lay'd[65] full low   405
  (")The harmless Albatross.

1817

The Polar
Spirit's fellow-
dæmons,
the invisible
inhabitants
of the element,
take part in the[66]
wrong; and
two of them
relate, one to
the other, that
penance long
and heavy for
the ancient
Mariner hath been accorded to the Polar Spirit, who returneth southward.

How long in that same fit I lay,
  I have not to declare;
But ere my living life returned,
I heard and in my soul discerned
  Two VOICES in the air.   400

"Is it he?" quoth one, "Is this the man?
By him who died on cross,
With his cruel bow he laid full low,
The harmless Albatross.   405

---

[64] In 1805 this is a quotation within a quotation, though there are quotation marks only for the beginning and ending.
[65] 1805 reads "laid."
[66] Marked through; "his" written in, *YSL*; 1828 prints "his."

1798

    "The spirit who 'bideth by himself
    "In the land of mist and snow,
    "He lov'd the bird that lov'd the man
    "Who shot him with his bow.

    The other was a softer voice,   420
      As soft as honey-dew:
    Quoth he the man hath penance done,
      And penance more will do.

1800

    (")The <S>pirit who (')bideth by himself
    (")In the land of mist and snow,
    (")He lov<e>d the bird that lov<e>d the man
    (")Who shot him with his bow.(")   410

    The other was a softer voice,
      As soft as honey-dew:
    Quoth he<, 'T>he man hath penance done,
      And penance more will do.<'>

1817

    The spirit who bideth by himself
    In the land of mist and snow,
    He loved the bird that loved the man
    Who shot him with his bow."

    The other was a softer voice,   410
    As soft as honey-dew:
    Quoth he, "The man hath penance done,
    And penance more will do."

1798

VI.

FIRST VOICE.

"But tell me, tell me! speak again,
  "Thy soft response renewing—   425
"What makes that ship drive on so fast?
  "What is the Ocean doing?

1800

VI.

FIRST VOICE.

"<'>⁶⁷But tell me, tell me! speak again,   415
  (")Thy soft response renewing—
(")What makes that ship drive on so fast?
  (")What is the Ocean doing?<'>

1817

THE RIME OF THE ANCIENT MARINER.
PART THE SIXTH.

FIRST VOICE.

|"|BUT tell me, tell me! speak again,
Thy soft response renewing—   415
What makes that ship drive on so fast?
What is the OCEAN doing?|"|

---

⁶⁷ Only one set of quotation marks in all but 1805.

1798

SECOND VOICE.

"Still as a Slave before his Lord,
  "The Ocean hath no blast:
"His great bright eye most silently   430
  "Up to the moon is cast —

"If he may know which way to go,
  "For she guides him smooth or grim.
"See, brother, see! how graciously
  "She looketh down on him.   435

1800

SECOND VOICE.

(")<'>Still as a Slave before his Lord,
  (")The Ocean hath no blast:
(")His great bright eye most silently   420
  (")Up to the moon is cast —

(")If he may know which way to go,
  (")For she guides him smooth or grim.
(")See, brother, see! how graciously
  (")She looketh down on him.<'>   425

1817

SECOND VOICE.

|"|Still as a slave before his lord,
The OCEAN hath no blast;
His great bright eye most silently   420
Up to the Moon is cast —

If he may know which way to go|,|/;/
For she guides him smooth or grim.
See, brother, see! how graciously
She looketh down on him.|"| 425

1798

FIRST VOICE.

"But why drives on that ship so fast
"Withouten wave or wind?

SECOND VOICE.

"The air is cut away before,
"And closes from behind.

1800

FIRST VOICE.

(")<'>But why drives on that ship so fast
(")Without or wave or wind?<'>

SECOND VOICE.

(")<'>The air is cut away before,
(")And closes from behind.

430

1817

The Mariner
hath been
cast into a
trance; for
the angelic
power
causeth the
vessel to drive
northward,
faster than
human life
could endure.

FIRST VOICE.

But why drives on that ship so fast,
Without or wave or wind?

SECOND VOICE.

The air is cut away before,
And closes from behind.

1798

> "Fly, brother, fly! more high, more high,   440
>   "Or we shall be belated:
> "For slow and slow that ship will go,
>   "When the Marinere's trance is abated."
>
> I woke, and we were sailing on
>   As in a gentle weather: 445
> 'Twas night, calm night, the moon was high;
>   The dead men stood together.

_____

1800

> (")Fly, brother, fly! more high, more high,
>   (")Or we shall be belated:
> (")For slow and slow that ship will go,
>   (")When the Mariner's trance is abated.(")<'>
>
> <">I woke, and we were sailing on   435
>   As in a gentle weather:
> 'Twas night, calm night, the moon was high;
>   The dead men stood together.

_____

1817

> Fly, brother, fly! more high, more high!   430
> Or we shall be belated:
> For slow and slow that ship will go,
> When the Mariner's trance is abated.
>
> I woke, and we were sailing on[68]
> As in a gentle weather:
> 'Twas night, calm night, the Moon was high;   435
> The dead men stood together.

The supernatural motion is retarded; the Mariner awakes, and his penance begins anew.

_____

[68] Coleridge crosses out the quotation mark beginning this line, along with all those in the voices' exchange, *YSL*.

1798

> All stood together on the deck,
>   For a charnel-dungeon fitter:
> All fix'd on me their stony eyes   450
>   That in the moon did glitter.
>
> The pang, the curse, with which they died,
>   Had never pass'd away:
> I could not draw my een from theirs
>   Ne turn them up to pray.   455

1800

> All stood together on the deck,   440
>   For a charnel-dungeon fitter:
> All fix<e>d on me their stony eyes
>   That in the moon did glitter.
>
> The pang, the curse, with which they died,
>   Had never pass<e>d away;
> I could not draw my eyes from theirs<,>   445
>   Nor turn them up to pray.

1817

> All stood together on the deck,
> For a charnel-dungeon fitter:
> All fixed on me their stony eyes,   440
> That in the Moon did glitter.
>
> The pang, the curse, with which they died,
> Had never passed away:
> I could not draw my eyes from theirs,
> Nor turn them up to pray.   445

1798

And in its time the spell was snapt,
  And I could move my een:
I look'd far-forth, but little saw
  Of what might else be seen.

Like one, that on a lonely road   460
  Doth walk in fear and dread,
And having once turn'd round, walks on
  And turns no more his head:
Because he knows, a frightful fiend
  Doth close behind him tread.   465

1800

And[69] now this spell was snapt: once more
  I view<e>d the ocean green,
And look<e>d far forth, yet little saw
  Of what had else been seen —   450

Like one, that on a lonesome road
  Doth walk in fear and dread,
And having once turn<e>d round, walks on
  And turns no more his head(:)<;>
Because he knows, a frightful fiend   455
  Doth close behind him tread.

1817

And now this spell was snapt: once more   The curse is
I viewed the ocean green,   finally
And looked far forth, yet little saw   expiated.
Of what had else been seen —

Like one, that on a lonesome road   450
Doth walk in fear and dread,
And having once turned round, walks on,
And turns no more his head;
Because he knows, a frightful fiend
Doth close behind him tread.   455

---

[69] "But" appears cancelled in the line above. See Griggs I:601.

1798

But soon there breath'd a wind on me,
  Ne sound ne motion made:
Its path was not upon the sea
  In ripple or in shade.

It rais'd my hair, it fann'd my cheek,   470
  Like a meadow-gale of spring—
It mingled strangely with my fears,
  Yet it felt like a welcoming.

1800

But soon there breath\<e>d a wind on me,
  Nor sound nor motion made:
Its path was not upon the sea
  In ripple or in shade.   460

It rais\<e>d my hair, it fann\<e>d my cheek,
  Like a meadow-gale of spring—
It mingled strangely with my fears,
  Yet it felt like a welcoming.

1817

But soon there breathed a wind on me,
  Nor sound nor motion made:
Its path was not upon the sea,
  In ripple or in shade.

It raised my hair, it fanned my cheek   460
Like a meadow-gale of spring—
It mingled strangely with my fears,
  Yet it felt like a welcoming.

1798

Swiftly, swiflty flew the ship,
  Yet she sail'd softly too: 475
Sweetly, sweetly blew the breeze —
  On me alone it blew.

O dream of joy! is this indeed
  The light-house top I see?
Is this the Hill? Is this the Kirk?   480
  Is this mine own countrée?

1800

Swiftly, swiftly flew the ship,   465
  Yet she sail<e>d softly too:
Sweetly, sweetly blew the breeze —
  On me alone it blew.

O dream of joy! is this indeed
  The light-house top I see?   470
Is this the Hill? Is this the Kirk?
  Is this mine own countrée?

1817

Swiftly, swiftly flew the ship,
Yet she sailed softly too: 465
Sweetly, sweetly blew the breeze —
On me alone it blew.

O/!/ dream of joy! is this indeed   And the an-
The light-house top I see?   cient Mariner
Is this the hill? is this the kirk?   beholdeth his
Is this mine own countrée?   native   470
                                    country.

1798

> We drifted o'er the Harbour-bar,
>   And I with sobs did pray —
> "O let me be awake, my God!
>   "Or let me sleep alway!"   485
>
> The harbour-bay was clear as glass,
>   So smoothly it was strewn!
> And on the bay the moon light lay,
>   And the shadow of the moon.

1800

> We drifted o'er the Harbour-bar,
>   And I with sobs did pray —
> (")<'>O let me be awake, my God!   475
>   (")Or let me sleep alway!(")<'>
>
> The harbour-bay was clear as glass,
>   So smoothly it was strewn!
> And on the bay the moonlight lay,
>   And the shadow of the moon.   480

1817

> We drifted o'er the harbour-bar,
>   And I with sobs did pray —
> O let me be awake, my God!
>   Or let me sleep alway.   475
>
> The harbour-bay was clear as glass,
>   So smoothly it was strewn!
> And on the bay the moonlight lay,
>   And the shadow of the moon.

1798

The moonlight bay was white all o'er,   490
  Till rising from the same,
Full many shapes, that shadows were,
  Like as of torches came.

A little distance from the prow
  Those dark-red shadows were;   495
But soon I saw that my own flesh
  Was red as in a glare.

1800

1817

1798

I turn'd my head in fear and dread,
  And by the holy rood,
The bodies had advanc'd, and now   500
  Before the mast they stood.

They lifted up their stiff right arms,
  They held them strait and tight;
And each right-arm burnt like a torch,
  A torch that's borne upright.   505
Their stony eye-balls glitter'd on
  In the red and smoky light.

1800

1817

1798

I pray'd and turn'd my head away
  Forth looking as before.
There was no breeze upon the bay,   510
  No wave against the shore.

The rock shone bright, the kirk no less
  That stands above the rock:
The moonlight steep'd in silentness
  The steady weathercock.   515

1800

The rock shone bright, the kirk no less
  That stands above the rock:
The moonlight steep<e>d in silentness
  The steady weathercock.

1817

The rock shone bright, the kirk no less,   480
That stands above the rock:
The moonlight steeped in silentness
The steady weathercock.

1798

And the bay was white with silent light,
  Till rising from the same
Full many shapes, that shadows were,
  In crimson colours came.   520

A little distance from the prow
  Those crimson shadows were:
I turn'd my eyes upon the deck —
  O Christ! what saw I there?

1800

And the bay was white with silent light,   485
  Till rising from the same
Full many shapes, that shadows were,
  In crimson colours came.

A little distance from the prow
  Those crimson shadows were: 490
I turn<e>d my eyes upon the deck —
  O Christ! what saw I there?

1817

And the bay was white with silent light,
Till rising from the same,   485
Full many shapes, that shadows were,
In crimson colours came.

And appear   A little distance from the prow
in their own   Those crimson shadows were:
forms of light. I turned my eyes upon the deck —   490
  Oh! Christ! what saw I there!

1798

> Each corse lay flat, lifeless and flat;   525
>   And by the Holy rood
> A man all light, a seraph-man,
>   On every corse there stood.
>
> This seraph-band, each wav'd his hand:
>   It was a heavenly sight: 530
> They stood as signals to the land,
>   Each one a lovely light:

1800

> Each corse lay flat, lifeless and flat;
>   And by the Holy rood
> A man all light, a seraph-man,   495
>   On every corse there stood.
>
> This seraph-band, each wav<e>d his hand:
>   It was a heavenly sight:
> They stood as signals to the land,
>   Each one a lovely light: 500

1817

> Each corse lay flat, lifeless and flat,
> And, by the holy rood!
> A man all light, a seraph-man,
> On every corse there stood.   495
>
> This seraph-band, each waved his hand:
> It was a heavenly sight!
> They stood as signals to the land,
> Each one a lovely[70] light;[71]

---

[70] "Heavenly" crossed through, *YSL*.
[71] The text of "The Rime of the Ancient Mariner" ends here in *YSL* with Coleridge's signature, and directions to Gutch (to refer) to "Small Sheet/ Bristol." This is page 32. The facing page is the Greek epigraph for "Ode to The Departing Year." The next numbered page is the first with text of the "Ode," page 51.

1798

This seraph-band, each wav'd his hand,
  No voice did they impart —
No voice; but O! the silence sank,   535
  Like music on my heart.

Eftsones I heard the dash of oars,
  I heard the pilot's cheer:
My head was turn'd perforce away
  And I saw a boat appear.   540

1800

This seraph-band, each wav\<e\>d his hand,
  No voice did they impart —
No voice; but O! the silence sank(,)
  Like music on my heart.

But soon I heard the dash of oars,   505
  I heard the pilot's cheer:
My head was turn\<e\>d perforce away\<,\>
  And I saw a boat appear.

1817

This seraph-band, each waved his hand,   500
No voice did they impart —
No voice; but oh! the silence sank
Like music on my heart.

But soon I heard the dash of oars,
I heard the Pilots's cheer;   505
My head was turn|e|d perforce away,
And I saw a boat appear.

1798

    Then vanish'd all the lovely lights;
      The bodies rose anew:
    With silent pace, each to his place,
      Came back the ghastly crew.
    The wind, that shade nor motion made,   545
      On me alone it blew.

        Then vanish'd all the lovely ligh[ts,]
          The spirits of the air;
        No souls of mortal men we[re]/ they[,]
          But spirits bright and fair.[72]   550

1800

1817

---

    [72]This variant stanza appears in very faint pencil at the bottom of 43 in the Bristol *LB* (#2603). The final words of the first and third lines are cut off by the edge of the page; "they" appears below the line, and the comma is so faint as to be almost conjectural.

1798

The pilot, and the pilot's boy
  I heard them coming fast:
Dear Lord in Heaven! it was a joy,
  The dead men could not blast.

I saw a third — I heard his voice: 555
  It is the Hermit good!
He singeth loud his godly hymns
  That he makes in the wood.
He'll shrieve my soul, he'll wash away
  The Albatross's blood.   560

1800

The pilot, and the pilot's boy<,>
  I heard them coming fast: 510
Dear Lord in Heaven! it was a joy(,)
  The dead men could not blast.

I saw a third — I heard his voice:
  It is the Hermit good!
He singeth loud his godly hymns   515
  That he makes in the wood.
He'll shrieve my soul, he'll wash away
  The Albatross's blood.

1817

The Pilot, and the Pilot's boy,
I heard them coming fast:
Dear Lord in Heaven! it was a joy   510
The dead men could not blast.

I saw a third — I heard his voice:
It is the Hermit good!
He singeth loud his godly hymns
That he makes in the wood.   515
He'll shrieve my soul, he'll wash away
The Albatross's blood.

1798

VII.

This Hermit good lives in that wood
  Which slopes down to the Sea.
How loudly his sweet voice he rears!
He loves to talk with Marineres
  That come from a far Contrée.   565

1800

VII.

<">This Hermit good lives in that wood   520
  Which slopes down to the Sea.
How loudly his sweet voice he rears!
He loves to talk with Mariners
  That come from a far countrée.

1817

THE RIME OF THE ANCIENT MARINER.[73]
PART THE SEVENTH.

The Hermit
of the Wood,
     THIS Hermit good lives in that wood
     Which slopes down to the sea.
     How loudly his sweet voice he rears!   520
     He loves to talk with marineres
     That come from a far countrée.

---

[73] 1828 prints "THE ANCIENT MARINER."

1798

He kneels at morn and noon and eve —
 He hath a cushion plump:
It is the moss, that wholly hides
 The rotted old Oak-stump.

The Skiff-boat ne'rd: I heard them talk,   570
 "Why, this is strange, I trow!
"Where are those lights so many and fair
 "That signal made but now?

1800

He kneels at morn and noon and eve —
 He hath a cushion plump:
It is the moss,[74] that wholly hides   525
 The rotted old Oak-stump.

The Skiff-boat ner'd: I heard them talk,
 (")<'>Why, this is strange, I trow!
(")Where are those lights so many and fair
 (")That signal made but now?<'>   530

1817

He kneels at morn, and noon and eve —
 He hath a cushion plump:
It is the moss that wholly hides   525
 The rotted old oak-stump.

The Skiff-boat near/e/d: I heard them talk,
 "Why, this is strange, I trow!
Where are those lights so many and fair,
 That signal made but now?"   530

---

[74] No comma 1802, 1805.

1798

> "Strange, by my faith! the Hermit said —
> "And they answer'd not our cheer.   575
> "The planks look warp'd, and see those sails
> "How thin they are and sere!
> "I never saw aught like to them
> "Unless perchance it were

1800

> (")<'>Strange, by my faith!<'> the Hermit said —
> (")<'>And they answer<e>d not our cheer.
> (")The planks look warp<e>d, and see those sails
> (")How thin they are and sere!
> (")I never saw aught like to them   535
> (")Unless perchance it were

1817

> "Strange, by my faith!" the Hermit said —   Approacheth
> "And they answered not our cheer!   the ship with
> The planks looked warped! and see those sails,   wonder.
> How thin they are and sere!
> I never saw aught like to them,   535
> Unless perchance it were

1798

"The skeletons of leaves that lag   580
  "My forest-brook along:
"When the Ivy-tod is heavy with snow,
"And the Owlet whoops to the wolf below
  "That eats the she-wolf's young.

"Dear Lord! it has a fiendish look—   585
  (The Pilot made reply)
"I am a-fear'd.—"Push on, push on!
  "Said the Hermit cheerily.

1800

(")The skeletons of leaves that lag
  (")My forest brook along:
(")When the Ivy-tod is heavy with snow,
(")And the Owlet whoops to the wolf below   540
  (")That eats the she-wolf's young.(")<'>

(")<'>Dear lord! it has a fiendish look—
  (The Pilot made reply)[75]
(")I am a[-]fear<e>d.(")<'>—(")<'>Push on, push on!(")<'>
  Said the Hermit cheerily.   545

1817

The[76] skeletons of leaves that lag
My forest-brook along|:|/;/
When the ivy-tod is heavy with snow,
And the owlet whoops to the wolf below,   540
That eats the she-wolf's young."

/"/Dear Lord! it hath a fiendish look—
(The Pilot made reply)
I am a-feared/"/—/"/Push on, push on!/"/
Said the Hermit cheerily.   545

---

[75] Parenthesis in the text.
[76] For *The* read *Brown* (errata, *SL* 237). 1828 prints "Brown."

1798

> The Boat came closer to the Ship,
>   But I ne spake ne stirr'd!
> The Boat came close beneath the Ship,
>   And strait a sound was heard!   590
>
> Under the water it rumbled on,
>   Still louder and more dread:
> It reach'd the Ship, it split the bay;   595
>   The Ship went down like lead.

1800

> The Boat came closer to the Ship,
>   But I nor spake nor stirr<e>d(!)<:>
> The Boat came close beneath the Ship,
>   And strait⁷⁷ a sound was heard(!)<.>   550
>
> Under the water it rumbled on,
>   Still louder and more dread:
> It reach<e>d the (S)hip, it split the bay;
>   The (S)hip went down like lead.

1817

> The boat came closer to the ship,
> But I nor spake nor stirred;
> The boat came close beneath the ship,
> And straight a sound was heard.
>
> Under the water it rumbled on,   The ship   550
> Still louder and more dread: suddenly
> It reach[e]d the ship, it split the bay; sinketh.
> The ship went down like lead.

---

⁷⁷ 1805 prints "straight."

1798

Stunn'd by that loud and dreadful sound,
  Which sky and ocean smote:
Like one that had been seven days drown'd
  My body lay afloat:
But, swift as dreams, myself I found   600
  Within the Pilot's boat.

Upon the whirl, where sank the Ship,
  The boat spun round and round:
And all was still, save that the hill
  Was telling of the sound.   605

1800

Stunn<e>d by that loud and dreadful sound,   555
  Which sky and ocean smote(:)<,>
Like one that had been seven days drown<e>d
  My body lay afloat:
But, swift as dreams, myself I found
  Within the Pilot's boat.   560

Upon the whirl, where sank the Ship,
  The boat spun round and round\:\[,]
And all was still, save that the hill
  Was telling of the sound.

1817

The ancient
Mariner is
saved in the
Pilot's boat.

Stunned by that loud and dreadful sound,
  Which sky and ocean smote,   555
Like one that hath been seven days drown/e/d|,|
  My body lay afloat;
But swift as dreams, myself I found
  Within the Pilot's boat.

Upon the whirl, where sank the ship,   560
  The boat spun round and round;
And all was still, save that the hill
  Was telling of the sound.

1798

> I mov'd my lips: the Pilot shriek'd
>   And fell down in a fit.
> The Holy Hermit rais'd his eyes
>   And pray'd where he did sit.
>
> I took the oars: the Pilot's boy,   610
>   Who now doth crazy go,
> Laugh'd loud and long, and all the while
>   His eyes went to and fro,
> "Ha! ha!" quoth he — "full plain I see,
>   "The devil knows how to row."   615

1800

> I mov<e>d my lips: the Pilot shriek<e>d   565
>   And fell down in a fit.
> The Holy Hermit rais<e>d his eyes
>   And pray<e>d where he did sit.
>
> I took the oars: the Pilot's boy,
>   Who now doth crazy go,   570
> Laugh<e>d loud and long, and all the while
>   His eyes went to and fro,
> (")<'>Ha! ha!(")<'> quoth he — (")<'>full plain I see,
>   (")The devil knows how to row.(")<'>

1817

> I moved my lips — the Pilot shrieked
> And fell down in a fit;   565
> The holy Hermit raised his eyes,
> And prayed where he did sit.
>
> I took the oars: the Pilot's boy,
> Who now doth crazy go,
> Laughed loud and long, and all the while   570
> His eyes went to and fro.
> "Ha! ha!" quoth he, "full plain I see,
> The Devil knows how to row."

1798

And now all in mine own Countrée
 I stood on the firm land!
The Hermit stepp'd forth from the boat,
 And scarcely he could stand.

"O shrieve me, shrieve me, holy Man!   620
 The Hermit cross'd his brow —
"Say quick," quoth he, "I bid thee say
 "What manner man art thou?

1800

And now all in mine own (C)ountrée   575
 I stood on the firm land!
The Hermit stepp<e>d forth from the boat,
 And scarcely he could stand.

(")<'>O shrieve me, shrieve me, holy Man!(")<'>
 The Hermit cross<e>d his brow(—)<.>   580
(")<'>Say quick,(")<'> quoth he, <'>I bid thee say
 (")What manner man art thou?(")<'>

1817

                              And now, all in my own countrée,
                               I stood on the firm land!   575
                              The Hermit stepped forth from the boat,
                               And scarcely he could stand.

The ancient   "O shrieve me, shrieve me, holy man!"
Mariner   The Hermit crossed his brow.
earnestly   "Say quick," quoth he, "I bid thee say —   580
entreateth   What manner of man art thou?"
the Hermit
to shrieve
him; and the
penance of
life falls on
him.

1798

Forthwith this frame of mine was wrench'd
  With a woeful agony,
Which forc'd me to begin my tale
  And then it left me free.

625

Since then at an uncertain hour,
  Now oftimes and now fewer,
That anguish comes and makes me tell
  My ghastly aventure.

630

1800

Forthwith this frame of mind was wrench<e>d
  With a woeful agony,
Which forc<e>d me to begin my tale<,>
  And then it left me free.

585

Since then<,> at an uncertain hour(,)
  That agony[78] returns,<;>
And till my ghastly [T]ale is told(,)
  This[79] heart within me burns.

590

1817

Forthwith this frame of mine was wrench/e/d
With a woeful agony,
Which forced me to begin my tale;
And then it left me free.

585

Since then, at an uncertain hour,
That agony returns;
And till my ghastly tale is told,
This heart within me burns.

And ever
and anon
throughout
his future life
an agony
constraineth
him to travel
from land to
land,

---

[78] 1800 prints "agency." "Agony" appears in Griggs I:601.
[79] "My" appears cancelled in line above; Griggs I:601.

1798

I pass, like night, from land to land;
  I have strange power of speech;
The moment that his face I see
I know the man that must hear me;   635
  To him my tale I teach.

1800

I pass, like night, from land to land;
  I have strange power of speech;
The moment that his face I see
I know the man that must hear me;   595
  To him my tale I teach.

1817

I pass, like night, from land to land;   590
I have strange power of speech;
That moment that his face I see,
I know the man that must hear me:
To him my tale I teach.

1798

What loud uproar bursts from that door!
  The Wedding-guests are there;
But in the Garden-bower the Bride
  And Bride-maids singing are: 640
And hark the little Vesper-bell
  Which biddeth me to prayer.

O Wedding-guest! this soul hath been
  Alone on a wide wide sea:
So lonely 'twas, that God himself   645
  Scarce seemed there to be.

1800

What loud uproar bursts from that door!
  The (W)edding-guests are there;
But in the (G)arden-bower the (B)ride
  And the (B)ride-maids singing are\:\[;]
And hark the little (V)esper-bell   600
  Which biddeth me to prayer.

O (W)edding-guest! this soul hath been
  Alone on a wide wide sea:
So lonely 'twas, that God himself
  Scarce seemed there to be.   605

1817

What loud uproar bursts from that door!   595
The wedding-guests are there|;|/:/
But in the garden-bower the bride
And bride-maids singing are;
And hark the little vesper bell,
Which biddeth me to prayer!   600

O Wedding-Guest! this soul hath been
Alone on a wide wide sea:
So lonely 'twas, that God himself
Scarce seemed there to be.

1798

O sweeter than the Marriage-feast,
  'Tis sweeter far to me
To walk together to the Kirk
  With a goodly company.   650

To walk together to the Kirk
  And all together pray,
While each to his great Father bends,
Old men, and babes, and loving friends,
  And Youths, and Maidens gay.   655

1800

O sweeter than the (M)arriage-feast,
  'Tis sweeter far to me
To walk together to the Kirk
  With a goodly company(.)<: − >

To walk together to the Kirk   610
  And all together pray,
While each to his great (f)ather bends,
Old men, and babes, and loving friends,
  And (Y)ouths, and (M)aidens gay.

1817

O sweeter than the marriage-feast,   605
'Tis sweeter far to me,
To walk together to the kirk
With a goodly company! −

To walk together to the kirk,
And all together pray,   610
While each to his great Father bends,
Old men, and babes, and loving friends,
And youths and maidens gay!

1798

> Farewell, farewell! but this I tell
>   To thee, thou wedding-guest!
> He prayeth well who loveth well,[80]
>   Both man and bird and beast.
>
> He prayeth best who loveth best,   660
>   All things both great and small:
> For the dear God, who loveth us,
>   He made and loveth all.

1800

> Farewell, farewell! but this I tell   615
>   To thee, thou wedding-guest!
> He prayeth well who loveth well
>   Both man and bird and beast.
>
> He prayeth best who loveth best
>   All things both great and small: 620
> For the dear God, who loveth us,
>   He made and loveth all.<">

1817

> Farewell, farewell! but this I tell   And to teach
> To thee, thou Wedding-Guest!   by his own   615
> He prayeth well, who loveth well   example,
> Both man and bird and beast.   love and
>   reverence to
>   all things
> He prayeth best, who loveth best   that God
> All things both great and small;   made and
> For the dear God who loveth us,   loveth.
> He made and loveth all."   620

---

[80] Errata reads, "Omit the comma after 'loveth well.'" In the Wren Library copy of the Arch issue *LB* (#2604), the comma has been rubbed out.

1798

The Marinere, whose eye is bright,
  Whose beard with age is hoar,   665
Is gone; and now the wedding-guest
  Turn'd from the bridegroom's door.

He went, like one that hath been stunn'd
  And is of sense forlorn:
A sadder and a wiser man   670
  He rose the morrow morn.

1800

The Mariner, whose eye is bright,
  Whose beard with age is hoar,
Is gone; and now the wedding-guest   625
  Turn<e>d from the bridegroom's door.

He went, like one that hath been stunn<e>d
  And is of sense forlorn:
A sadder and a wiser man
  He rose the morrow morn.   630

1817

The Mariner, whose eye is bright,
Whose beard with age is hoar,
Is gone;/:/ and now the Wedding-Guest
Turned from the bridegroom's door.   625

He went like one that hath been stunned,
And is of sense forlorn:
A sadder and a wiser man,
He rose the morrow morn.

Commentary

The story of how Coleridge came to write "The Ancient Mariner" has taken its place as one of the key events of Romanticism. Wordsworth and Coleridge intended to collaborate on a ballad which they might sell to a magazine in order to pay for a planned walking tour. After a time the two poets diverged in their understanding of the poem, and Coleridge completed it on his own. This story generally appears in primers on Romanticism to signify the beginning of the *annus mirabilis* in which the two poets produced an overwhelming stock of poetry, resulting in the landmark *Lyrical Ballads* and a new age of literature. The full complex of events lying behind this partnership reveals, however, that the origin of Romanticism cannot be traced to a single explosive event. On the one hand, the history of "The Ancient Mariner" might be said to embrace the entire Romantic era, for, after its initial publication in 1798, Coleridge revised it repeatedly throughout the next three decades. On the other hand, the poem itself, thematically and through its extensive revisions, calls into question the legitimacy of assigning such status to any single narrative construction. The multifariousness of perspectives in the poem already raises the daunting question of how to ground historical knowledge in facts made tenuous through time and repeated scrutiny.

Because the lengthy process of its revision involves "The Ancient Mariner" in so much of Coleridge's life, the facts of the process open numerous avenues of understanding. From a strictly historical perspective, these facts — however sketchy they appear here — provide the context of Coleridge's changing attitude toward his poem. At the same time we must acknowledge that the compulsion to revise seemingly arises from the nature of the poem itself. A commentary on the texts of "The Ancient Mariner" ought to address both the factual history of the revisions and the compulsiveness of the poem which extends well beyond thematic concerns to shape the text. Thus the poem places two demands on a commentary which are in many ways philosophically opposed to one another. The tension of these opposing demands makes it all the more important that we attend to each one in turn. The following commentary therefore falls into two parts: the first provides the historical context of the poem and the second looks to the revisions themselves to uncover what has been silenced by traditional histories and standardized texts.

History of the Poem: Composition and Publication

Late in his life Wordsworth recounted how he and Coleridge, while walking through the Quantock Hills, "planned the poem of *The Ancient Mariner*, founded on a dream, as Mr. Coleridge said, of his friend Mr. Cruikshank."[1] Wordsworth goes on to tell how he

> had been reading in Shelvocke's *Voyages* a day or two before
> that, while doubling Cape Horn, [the sailors] frequently saw
> albatrosses in that latitude, the largest sort of sea-fowl, some
> extending their wings twelve or thirteen feet. "Suppose," said
> I, "you represent him as having killed one of these birds on
> entering the South Sea, and that the tutelary spirits of these
> regions take upon them to avenge the crime." The incident was
> thought fit for the purpose and adopted accordingly. I also
> suggested the navigation of the ship by the dead men, but do not
> recollect that I had anything more to do with the scheme of the
> poem. The gloss with which it was subsequently accompanied
> was not thought of by either of us at the time, at least not a hint
> of it was given to me, and I have no doubt it was a gratuitous
> afterthought.

Wordsworth goes on to indicate the "two or three lines" he contributed to the poem, and that his and Coleridge's "respective manners proved so widely different that it would have been quite presumptuous in me to do anything but separate from an undertaking upon which I could only have been a clog."

Elsewhere Wordsworth recounts that they "both determined to write some poetry for a monthly magazine, the profits of which were to defray the expenses of a little excursion we were to make together."[2] The "little excursion" seems to have been at first a tour "through Wales and northwards" and then to have become the trip to Germany he and Dorothy took with Coleridge the following year.[3] In this account Wordsworth also claims "The idea of 'shooting an albatross,'" and "the reanimation of the dead bodies, to work the ship."

Around 1830 Coleridge mentioned to his nephew, editor of *Table Talk*, that "at Porlock I wrote Christabel, and the Ancient Mariner."[4] On 13 November 1797, Dorothy records in her journal: "William and Coleridge employing themselves in laying the plan of a ballad; to be published with some pieces of William's" (*EY* 194). Seven days later Coleridge mentioned off-handedly to Joseph Cottle, "I have written a ballad of about 300 lines — & the Sketch of a Plan of General Study."[5] Other matters besides the trip to Germany were on his mind at this time, however, such as his penury. On the sixth of January 1798, he wrote to John Prior Estlin: "I am now utterly without money . . . I must borrow ten pound of you, 5£ of Mr Wade, and will sell my Ballad to Phillips who I doubt not will give me 5£ for it" (*CL* I:368). In February he writes to Cottle, "I have finished my ballad — it is 340 lines" (*CL* I:387), while the published poem was 658 lines.

Late in May of 1798, Coleridge sent a letter to Cottle concerned with the printing of *Lyrical Ballads*. Here he writes:

> We deem that the volumes offered to you are to a certain degree
> *one work*, in *kind tho' not in degree*, as an Ode is one work — &
> that our different poems are as stanzas, good relatively rather
> than absolutely: — Mark you, I say *in kind* tho' not in degree. —
> The extract from my Tragedy will have no sort of reference to
> my Tragedy, but is a Tale in itself, as the ancient Mariner. — The
> Tragedy will not be mentioned — (*CL* I:412)

This comment becomes especially significant in light of the fact that both poets came to look upon *Lyrical Ballads* as Wordsworth's exclusive property. Coleridge's statement here expresses an understanding of the collection in accord with the anonymity of its publication. At least from his perspective at this time, the volume

is truly a collaboration, belonging to neither poet exclusively. Coleridge's
comment to Cottle holds importance in another light as well. The collaboration on
the volume which cemented Wordsworth's poetic career appears to have begun as
a cooperative effort on one poem — "The Ancient Mariner." For whatever reason,
the collaboration shifted emphasis from one poem to a volume of poems, which
yet remained "to a certain degree *one work*." But even when, eighteen years later,
Coleridge further shifted emphasis of the dual effort from the poem to the book,
he still stressed the collaboration:

> The thought suggested itself (to which of us I do not recollect)
> that a series of poems might be composed of two sorts. In the
> one, the incidents were to be, in part at least, supernatural . . . .
> For the second class, subjects were to be chosen from ordinary
> life . . . . With this view I wrote the "Ancient Mariner," and was
> preparing among other poems, the "Dark Ladie," and the
> "Christabel," in which I should have more nearly realized my
> ideal, than I had done in my first attempt. But Mr. Wordsworth's
> industry had proved so much more successful, and the number
> of his poems so much greater, that my compositions, instead of
> forming a balance, appeared rather an interpolation of hetero-
> geneous matter. Mr. Wordsworth added two or three poems
> written in his own character, in the impassioned, lofty, and
> sustained diction, which is characteristic of his genius. In this
> form the "Lyrical Ballads" were published; and were presented
> by him, as an *experiment*.[6]

Even in reminiscence, what mattered to both poets was that the poem arose through
collaboration, that they both had a stake in it.[7]

The compelling motive for the two poets, at this juncture anyway, was financial.
Both of them needed money, and saw the publication as a sure source of income.
Coleridge hoped the profits would tide him over until the Wedgewood annuity
came through, while Wordsworth's inheritance was being withheld from him by
Lord Lowther.[8] At the end of April 1798, Dorothy writes: "Our present plan is to

go to Germany for a couple of years. William thinks it will be a great advantage to him to be acquainted with the German language; besides that translation is the most profitable of all works. He is about to publish some poems. He is to have twenty guineas for one volume, and he expects more than twice as much for another which is nearly ready for publishing" (*EY* 216). In fact, as she later recorded, he received thirty guineas for *Lyrical Ballads* (*EY* 227).[9]

According to Campbell, "The Wordsworths [Dorothy and William] had quitted Alfoxden at Midsummer, and, after staying a week with the Coleridges, they walked to Bristol, where they took lodgings, and superintended the printing of the *Lyrical Ballads*. Before the end of August they were in London in readiness for their journey."[10] The Wordsworths and Coleridge left for Germany on the fourteenth of September, and *Lyrical Ballads, with a few other Poems* "had been published a few days before."[11]

Campbell's account elides a number of significant details. Biggs and Cottle had already printed the volume when it was decided (by whom remains unclear) to substitute "The Nightingale" for "Lewti," apparently to preserve the anonymity of the volume since the latter was known to be Coleridge's. [12] It is possible furthermore that a few copies were circulated among friends, including Southey who warned Cottle the book would not sell. At this point the publication stalled while the printer's financial worries got the best of him. In September Cottle transferred *Lyrical Ballads* to the firm of J. and A. Arch of London, who published the volume on 4 October. The confusion over printing and distribution resulted in two separate issues of the volume: the first, under the imprint, "Printed by Biggs and Cottle, for T. N. Longman," contains "Lewti," while the second, "Printed for J. & A. Arch," contains "The Nightingale."[13] The confusion caused by the transfer led to a dispute over the copyright, which Wordsworth angrily claimed as his own (*EY* 259, 263, and 673-76).

The volume, which literary history has held as the landmark of a new age in poetry, received mixed reviews from its contemporaries. The anonymous reviewer for *British Critic* says of "The Ancyent Marinere" that "the beginning and the end are striking and well-conducted; but the intermediate part is too long," and states that the author "is confidently said to be Mr. Coleridge."[14] But for the most part, the volume was either ignored or reviewed badly, as in Southey's famous comment on "The Ancyent Marinere": "We do not sufficiently understand the story to analyse it. It is a Dutch attempt at German sublimity. Genius has here been employed in producing a poem of little merit."[15] And similarly the reviewer from the *Analytical Review* comments on the poem, "We are not pleased with it; in our opinion it has more of the extravagance of a mad german poet, than of the simplicity of our ancient ballad writers."[16] Though British readers were familiar with ballads and imitations of antique ballads throughout the 1790's, "The Rime of the Ancyent Marinere" seemed unlike anything they had ever encountered.[17] Most of the negative comments on the volume, furthermore, focussed on Coleridge's poem.

Wordsworth openly blamed "The Rime of the Ancyent Marinere" for the low sales of *Lyrical Ballads*: "From what I can gather it seems that The Ancyent Mariner has upon the whole been an injury to the volume, I mean that the old words and the strangeness of it have deterred readers from going on" (*EY* 264). Coleridge, however, claims he "was told by Longmans that the greater part of the Lyrical Ballads had been sold to seafaring men, who having heard of the Ancient Mariner, concluded that it was a naval song-book, or, at all events, that it had some relation to nautical matters."[18] On the eighth of June 1800, however, Wordsworth wrote to his brother Richard:

> The first edition of *Lyrical Ballads* is sold off and another is called for by the Booksellers, for the right of printing 2 editions of 750 each of this vol: of poems and of printing two editions, one of 1000 and another of 750 of another vol of the same size, I am offered by Longman 80£. I think I shall accept the offer as if the books sell quickly I shall soon have the right of going to market with them again when their merit will be known, and if they do not sell tolerably, Longman will have given enough for them. (*EY* 283)

The note which de Selincourt appends to this letter indicates that "It was no doubt S.T.C. who arranged with the Bristol firm of Biggs & Cottle to print the volumes, and . . . with Longman to be the publisher" (*EY* 283-84n). From the twenty-ninth of this same month to the twenty-third of July, Coleridge and Dorothy prepared a manuscript copy for the new edition of *Lyrical Ballads* to be published by Biggs and Cottle. Wordsworth felt too ill with pains in his side to contribute much during this month. At the end of July, when Coleridge left Grasmere for Keswick, Wordsworth wrote to Humphry Davy in Bristol, asking him to check the proof sheets (*EY* 289).

From this point until the publication, Wordsworth wrote a number of letters to the printers indicating changes he desired in his poems. His concern at this point was obsessive, as he often changed details several times; he required that the number of lines to a page be held to a maximum of eighteen, "or never more than 19 in a page as was done in the first Edition of *Lyrical Ballads*," apparently to ensure that the book reached the requisite minimum of 205 pages (*EY* 307). As Stephen Gill states, Wordsworth "had so completely taken control that *Lyrical Ballads* of 1800 bears only residual marks of the collaborative effort of 1798."[19] Wordsworth's name alone appeared on the title page, and he took responsibility for the Preface even though much later he disclaimed it: "I never cared a straw about the theory — & the Preface was written at the request of Coleridge out of sheer good nature — I recollect the very spot, a deserted Quarry in the Vale of Grasmere where he pressed the thing upon me, & but for that it would never have been thought of."[20] As Mark Reed shows, Wordsworth's poetic ambition found its character in the publication of *Lyrical Ballads*, while Coleridge's remained ill-defined.[21] Wordsworth, finding in *Lyrical Ballads* a poetic voice which appealed to the public sufficiently to found a poetic vocation, felt he had more at stake in the volume than Coleridge did, and so he made it his own. He took it over, though in the Preface he clearly demarcated his poems from Coleridge's, stating "for the sake of variety and from a consciousness of my own weakness I was induced to request the assistance of a Friend."[22] The "Friend" remains significantly and troublingly anonymous.

In early October of 1800 Wordsworth informed Biggs and Cottle that it was his "wish and determination that (whatever the expence may be, which I hereby take upon myself) such Pages of the Poem of Christabel as have been printed (if any such there be) be cancelled — I wish to have other poems substituted" (*EY* 305). In the middle of December, he followed up this command with another letter to the printers:

> A Poem of Mr Coleridge's was to have concluded the Volumes;
> but upon mature deliberation I found that the Style of this Poem
> was so discordant from my own that it could not be printed along
> with my poems with any propriety. I had other poems by me of
> my own which would have been sufficient for our purpose but
> some of them being connected with political subjects I judged
> that they would be injurious to the sale of the Work. I therefore,
> since my last letter, wrote the last poem of the 2nd Volume. I
> am sure when you see the work you will approve of this delay,
> as there can be no doubt that the poem alluded to will be highly
> serviceable to the Sale. (*EY* 309)

The poem Wordsworth wished to delete was "Christabel," and the one replacing
it was "Michael." The story of "Christabel" directly relates to the history of "The
Ancient Mariner," in that it shows the extent to which Wordsworth increasingly
envisioned *Lyrical Ballads* as his own property.

Gill argues that the primary reason Wordsworth treated Coleridge so un-
graciously, especially in regard to "Christabel," was his "overmastering determi-
nation to speak to the public in his own voice, with a volume of poems which should
exhibit a coherent identity and unignorable seriousness of purpose."[23] Wordsworth's
determination also involved merely pecuniary aims, for *Lyrical Ballads* had
proven valuable "as a commercial product to be marketed."[24] Wordsworth's
objections to Coleridge's contributions, but especially "The Ancient Mariner" and
"Christabel," show that commercial success helped to determine the integrity of
his voice. Even in June 1799, a year before Coleridge negotiated for the second
edition, Wordsworth wrote to Cottle: "I should very much wish to know what
number of the poems have been sold, and also (as, if the edition should sell, I shall
probably add some others in Lieu of the Ancyent Marinere) what we are to do with
the Copy Right. I repeat this that it may not be overlooked when you write to me"
(*EY* 263).

I dwell on the point of Wordsworth's claim to *Lyrical Ballads* because he
convinced Coleridge to make the numerous changes to "The Ancyent Marinere"
after the first edition. His aim of a "coherent identity" was focussed on public

expectation and profit rather than the intention to revolutionize British poetry. As his angry dispute over the copyright shows, Wordsworth early on appropriated *Lyrical Ballads* as his product, and was concerned with the effect of Coleridge's poem for that reason. He was clearly not interested in continuing with the experiment of collaboration or of allowing divergent voices to appear with his own. In looking to a career as a poet, Wordsworth understood that he needed to mold a recognizable persona that would interest the public enough to continue buying his poems. He increasingly thought of *Lyrical Ballads* as the solidification of his poetic career — more so than, say, *Descriptive Sketches* — and so left off trying to add "variety" or any recognition of his "own weakness."[25]

In July of 1800 Coleridge sent a pair of letters to Biggs and Cottle with instructions on his revisions of "The Ancient Mariner" for the new edition. The alterations are extensive, beginning with the title, which changes from "The Rime of the Ancyent Marinere" to "The Ancient Mariner, A Poet's Reverie," and continuing with modernized spelling, and deleted, added, or changed stanzas. But the alterations did not mollify Wordsworth, who insisted on prefacing the poem with the following statement:

> I cannot refuse myself the gratification of informing such Readers as may have been pleased with this poem, or with any part of it, that they owe their pleasure in some sort to me; as the Author was himself very desirous that it should be suppressed. This wish had arisen from a consciousness of the poem, & from a knowledge that many persons had been much displeased with it. The Poem of my Friend has indeed great defects; first that the principal person has no distinct character, either in his profession of Mariner, or as a human being who having been long under the controul of supernatural impressions might be supposed himself to partake of something supernatural: secondly, that he does not act, but is continually acted upon: Thirdly, that the events having no necessary connection do not produce each other; and lastly, that the imagery is somewhat too laboriously accumulated. Yet the poem contains many delicate

touches of passion, and indeed the passion is every where true
to nature; a great number of the stanzas present beautiful images
& are expressed with unusual felicity of language; and the
versification, though the metre is itself unfit for long poems, is
harmonious and artfully varied, exhibiting the utmost powers of
that metre, & every variety of which it is capable. It therefore
appeared to me that these several merits (the first of which,
namely that of the passion, is of the highest kind) gave to the
poem a value which is not often possessed by better poems. On
this account I requested my Friend to permit me to republish it.
(*CL* I:602)

Considering how forcefully Wordsworth appropriated *Lyrical Ballads*, his defense
of the poem is disingenuously self-serving. While congratulating himself for
recognizing the "several merits" of "The Ancient Mariner," he makes plain that
the poem is not his, and does not fit in with the effect he desires for the volume.
The "defects" he lists highlight the particular qualities he seeks in his own poems.
The variety he has sought in including the poems of his friend appears to have been
that of weakness contrasting strength. In effect, then, he is disavowing responsi-
bility for "The Ancient Mariner" to make *Lyrical Ballads* more completely his
own.

   The second edition of *Lyrical Ballads* appeared in two volumes on 25 January
1801 (*EY* 317n). No longer holding the lead-off position, as it had in the single-
volume 1798 edition, Coleridge's poem stood at the end of volume one. By June
of 1801, only 130 copies were left unsold, and Longman invited Wordsworth to
prepare a new edition. There is no indication that Wordsworth consulted Coleridge
for this revision, but his own changes were extensive, even though they primarily
affected punctuation, spelling, and short phrases. His note on "The Ancient
Mariner" was dropped, while the poem retained its position at the end of volume
one in the two subsequent editions of *Lyrical Ballads*, of 1802 and 1805. In each
of these editions, numerous changes appeared in the poem, primarily in spelling
and punctuation. Because Coleridge makes no recorded mention of these two
editions, (and because he would have been in Malta when work on the 1805 edition

was being done), we can conclude that the changes were made by Wordsworth. The fourth edition of *Lyrical Ballads* was the final one, and the last time "The Ancient Mariner" appeared in a collection of Wordsworth's poems.

In May of 1807 Coleridge mentioned in a letter to William Sotheby,

> I have made a contract with Mr Longman for 100 guineas to be paid me on the delivery of two volumes of poems — these are all ready, save only two — but these are the two that I cannot with propriety place any where but at the beginning of the first Volume, & I wish of course to give a week's correction & thought to the others — two months however are the utmost (death & sickness out of the question) that will intervene between this & the completion of my Contract. (*CL* III:15)

For this collection Coleridge apparently considered revising "The Ancient Mariner" in some direction, for the notebook entry of October 1806 shows his reworking of lines 205-217.[26] This was the same time in which Humphry Davy was trying to engage Coleridge for the series of lectures at the Royal Institution, and Josiah Wedgewood was inquiring after the contribution to the life of his brother Thomas which Coleridge had promised.[27] Of the contribution to the life of his friend, nothing came. The lectures were ultimately postponed until the following year, when he nonetheless cancelled at least two because of poor health. During much of the period following his return from Malta, Coleridge suffered from illness, attested to in almost every letter, though in fact the problem lay in the opium addiction, which had not lessened in Malta as he had hoped, but, indeed, seems to have worsened. In light of all these failed projects, his poor health, and the increasing guilt over his addiction, it is not surprising that his announcement of a publishing contract came to nought.

Again, however, in 1809 Coleridge corresponded with Longman to propose a new collection of his poetry. This time he envisioned a collection of three volumes: the first would consist of the 1803 *Poems*, to which Longman owned the copyright.[28] For the remaining volumes, Coleridge divided his poems into two different categories: those of sufficient length (i.e., when finished) to fill a volume on their own and which had never been published, and those already published, which "would with the notes make near 400 pages." Of the second group he goes on to say,

> But of these tho' all are my own property, yet several have already appeared, tho' very different from their present form, in the Morning Post—these however are of small consequence from their minor size etc.—and the A. Mariner (which in any future Edition Wordsworth will withdraw from the L. Ballads, now sold out) in the L.B.—

> . . . Now, as the first Volume is your *property*, I have no objection to dispose of the absolute Copyright of the second, or second & third . . . both for that reason, and in order that any defect of immediate novelty from the Ancient Mariner having past thro' several Editions in the L.B. . . . may be fully counterbalanced by the certainty of the whole advantage (whatever that may chance to be) derived from any present or future reputation. . . . (*CL* III:204)

Coleridge asked £120 for the copyright, though Longman offered him only a hundred. This offer apparently did not satisfy Coleridge, for he presented his poems anew to Longman in 1811. This time he received a twenty pound advance, but, as with the other negotiations with Longman, the deal was never completed (*CL* IV:324-25).

The first time "The Ancient Mariner" appeared under Coleridge's own name was in the 1817 *Sibylline Leaves*. While the poem had been moved to the end of the second volume in the 1800 *Lyrical Ballads*, it reverted back to the lead-off position in this new volume. In addition it changed titles again, from "The Ancient Mariner, A Poet's Reverie" to "The Rime of the Ancient Mariner, In Seven Parts." The most noticeable alteration, however, was the addition of the prose gloss.

When Coleridge actually composed the gloss is questionable. R. C. Bald indicates that two annotations in a copy of the 1800 *Lyrical Ballads* in Melbourne

Public Library confirm the opinion that the gloss was "composed ... comparatively soon after the original composition of the poem."[29] John Livingston Lowes points out that because of the time elapsed between the publication of *Lyrical Ballads* and that of *Sibylline Leaves*, there is every possibility that Coleridge composed the gloss much earlier than 1815. In addition, since the pages of *Sibylline Leaves* containing "The Ancient Mariner" were printed in 1815, the "courts of the sun" gloss might have been written even before the volume saw the light of publication.[30]

During Easter week of 1815, Coleridge wrote to Lord Byron that he had long "been urged – and my circumstances now compel me to publish in two Volumes all the poems composed by me from the year 1795 to the present Date." He goes on to state that these volumes would include

> the Poems published in the Lyrical Ballads and omitted in Mr
> Wordsworth's collection of all his minor poems, as was agreed
> on mutually by us – and which tho' much called for have been
> out of Print for some years, in consequence of Mr Wordsworth's
> determination not to re-edit the Lyrical ballads separately . . . .
> The whole have been corrected throughout, with very consider-
> able alterations and additions, some indeed almost re-written.
> (*CL* IV:560)

Among the changes, he lists "A Particular Preface to the Ancient Mariner and the Ballads on the employment of the Supernatural in Poetry and the Laws which regulate it – in answer to a note of Sir W. Scott's in the Lady of the Lake. Both volumes will be ready for the Press by the first week in June" (*CL* IV:561). The purpose of the letter is to request Byron's help in acquiring a publisher for the volumes, preferably not Longman with whom he was still on uneasy terms. Coleridge argues, reasonably, that with Byron's recommendation the volumes would bring "treble the amount" he could attract on his own. In September of the same year, Coleridge is writing to John May that he has delivered the manuscripts of two volumes (the first consisting of the *Biographia*, the second of the poems) to his printer, Mr. Gutch of Bristol (*CL* IV:588). Coleridge began sending copy to the printers in November 1815, at which time Gutch began printing in Bristol (*CL* IV:593, 618). The final proof sheets for *Sibylline Leaves* were sent off to Bristol 14 June 1816.

The publication history of *Sibylline Leaves* becomes complicated at this point because the collection was to have been published as the second volume of *Biographia Literaria*. In May, when Gutch saw he had miscalculated the length of printed sheets to be gotten from the manuscript, he decided to divide the *Biographia* into two volumes, so that *Sibylline Leaves* would make the third volume. Gutch requested that Coleridge add the 150 pages required to fill the second volume, but when Coleridge let three weeks pass before responding, the printer wrote a letter of complaint to Gillman — the physician into whose household Coleridge had moved in the attempt to curb his addiction. Coleridge responded with an angry letter (6 or 7 August 1816: *CL* IV:661-63) asking Gutch to send him an account of the costs incurred so that he might transfer the job to the London firm of Gale and Fenner.

A dispute over costs for the sheets already printed (which included the third volume, or *Sibylline Leaves*) arose. In March 1817 Gale and Fenner agreed to pay Gutch £265. 0s. 4d. for the printed sheets, but refused to pay Coleridge's debt to Gutch, so he had to borrow £28. In April the sheets arrived in London, but in a disarray that further slowed production. On 13 May 1817 Gale and Fenner wrote, "We have only just finished gathering and collating Coleridge's Life and Poems" (*CL* IV:659). Both *Biographia Literaria* and *Sibylline Leaves* were finally published by Gale and Fenner in July 1817, twenty months after printing began (*CL* IV:754).[31]

On 22 July 1817 Coleridge wrote to ask Thomas Poole to accept "a corrected copy of my Sibylline Leaves & Literary Life — and so wildly have they been printed, that a corrected Copy is of some value to those, to whom the works themselves are of any. I would, that the misprinting had been the worst of the delusions and ill-usage, to which my credulity exposed me from the said Printer" (*CL* IV:754). He did not get the chance to publish a corrected edition, for in March 1819 the firm of Rest and Fenner went bankrupt. This event forced Coleridge again to borrow money to buy up the unsold copies of his works (excepting *Biographia Literaria* and *Sibylline Leaves*, both of which "were bought at the private trade sale by a bookseller at a price not much below their trade value") along with the half copyrights owned by Fenner (*CL* IV:949). Further, Fenner had misrepresented the number of copies sold, thereby cheating Coleridge out of a considerable amount of money, which Coleridge estimated (though certainly with some exaggeration) to be as high as £1200 (*CL* IV:947).[32]

In the following spring of 1820, Coleridge mentioned that since the available copies of *Sibylline Leaves* "are all sold, & neither the Zapolya nor the Christabel are on sale," he might try to interest Longman in an edition of his collected poetry. A year later, in May of 1821, worried over his debt to Gillman, Coleridge mentioned to his son Derwent that he might "sell the copy-right of an Edition of my Poems, Biography, &c that have been long out of print" (*CL* V:140). By June of 1823 he still had not managed to interest anyone in an edition, though he requested his nephew, John Taylor Coleridge, to ask Murray if his firm would be interested. On 25 February 1827, however, he wrote to Daniel Stuart that "Mr Gillman and Mr [Robert] Jameson (the Chancery Barrister) have undertaken to superintend an Edition of all my Poems to be brought out by Pickering" (*CL* VI:672). This edition was *The Poetical Works of S. T. Coleridge, Including the Dramas of Wallenstein, Remorse, and Zapolya*, 3 vols. Apparently only 300 copies were printed by William Pickering, in August 1828, and sold off by October of that year (*CL* VI:766). This edition was reissued around May of 1829. "The Ancient Mariner" appeared at the beginning of volume two.

The poem appeared little changed in these late editions from its appearance in *Sibylline Leaves*. The changes were confined mostly to punctuation and spelling (often paralleling that of the 1805 *Lyrical Ballads*). One new gloss appeared in 1828, which had not been in the 1817 edition, commenting on the departure of the spectre ship. This gloss passed through at least four versions before reaching its final simple form, thus showing that Coleridge continued to tinker with details of his poem.[33]

The final edition of Coleridge's poetry appeared just prior to his death on 25 July 1834. Though Henry Nelson Coleridge superintended the publication, Coleridge himself handled many of the revisions. This edition apparently had been planned since 1832 as a cheaper one than the previous two (*CL* VI:923n). As with the other two published by Pickering, this one was in three volumes.

After Coleridge's death, the three-volume edition of 1834 was frequently reprinted. The next significant edition appeared in 1852, edited by Derwent and Sara Coleridge and published by Edward Moxon in London. The greater part of the work on this edition was performed by Sara Coleridge, including the preface and the notes. Derwent completed the edition after her death. In her preface Sara states that she based her edition on "those of 1817 and 1828, which may be held to represent the author's matured judgement upon the larger and more important part of his poetical productions. They have reason, indeed, to believe, that the edition of 1828 was the last upon which he was able to bestow personal care and attention. That of 1834, the last year of his earthly sojourning . . . was arranged mainly, if not entirely, at the discretion of his earliest Editor, H. N. Coleridge."[34]

In 1877 Basil Montagu issued a four-volume collection of the poetic and dramatic works. In 1885 T. Ashe published a two-volume edition. The edition of James Dykes Campbell appeared in 1893 with a biographical introduction and important notes to the poems. The poet's grandson, Earnest Hartley Coleridge, published the two-volume *Poetical Works* with Oxford University Press in 1912. This edition, based on the 1834 text, has remained the definitive edition of Coleridge's poetical works, to be superseded only when *The Collected Coleridge* produces its promised three-volume edition.

Significance of the Present Edition

Because Coleridge returned to "The Ancient Mariner" so recurrently throughout his life, the history of the poem can easily serve as a biographical reference point.[35] This story can prove very useful in establishing the factual, historical context which determined that the revisions proceed in one way rather than another. As Jerome McGann points out in his discussion of the poem, "meaning, in a literary event, is a function not of 'the poem itself' but of the poem's historical relations with its readers and interpreters."[36] McGann argues cogently that Coleridge's repeated alterations of the poem enact the development of many originally oral texts, such as "the Scriptures [which] grew by accretion and interpolation over an extended period of time. They do not represent a 'true' narrative of certain fixed original events; rather, they are a collection of poetic materials which represent the changing form of 'witness' or testament of faith created by a religious community in the course of its history."[37] Seen in this way, Coleridge's poem is no longer confined to the fictional account of an errant sailor, but can be said to integrate, through its thirty-year course of revisions, "the changing form" of Romanticism.

The present edition makes physically available the changing witness of the first decades of the nineteenth century. The facts traced in an historical account of the text constitute, according to McGann, the governing ideology in which the poem and its revisions occurred.[38] Among other issues, these facts raise the question of authority: as we shall see, this question only *begins* with textual authority, for the physical nature of this edition brings the question so forcefully into the open that it immediately expands into other areas of concern. The text, which enacts its own theme, questions all levels of authority, and, most powerfully, that claimed for any one edition and for the Mariner's identity.

Most of the editions of "The Ancient Mariner" published after Coleridge's death rely on the 1834 text, with the notable exception of the 1852 edition of Sara and Derwent Coleridge which follows the 1828 text. Traditional editorial principles dictate that either the last edition published in the author's lifetime, or the first edition published from manuscript should hold the privileged position of an authorized edition.[39] These views consider any change made by an author to be an improvement, or at least to have been intended as an improvement by the author. Both views are functions of the argument that the best edition of a literary work is the one which most accurately reflects the author's intentions. The accepted scholarly edition, that of E. H. Coleridge published in 1912, follows the 1834 edition, indicating many of the revisions in footnotes, and including the 1798 text in an appendix.[40] In sharp contrast to this standard is the edition of William Empson and David Pirie. They reject the claim that Coleridge's revisions improve upon the poem and state: "There is no logic in assuming that an author at the end of his life is the person best placed to grasp the essence of a poem written decades earlier," and therefore the "editor must clearly prevent an author from telling lies in the margin about the meaning of an early work."[41]

The present edition places itself somewhere between Empson and Pirie's view that an author does not know his work as well as an editor might and the traditional view that Coleridge knew his work more fully as time went on. To privilege one version over any other, or even the "eclectic" conglomeration that Empson and Pirie reconstruct, is to deny a basic quality of "The Ancient Mariner" itself. Probably more than any other literary work, "The Ancient Mariner" is shaped by the need to retell itself. The Mariner's endless wandering finds its analogy in the poem's endless textual recasting.

Throughout the long course of retellings, the Mariner's tale might be said to shift its emphasis somewhat, especially since its main character is so nebulous. We have no indication that any of his tellings is better than any of the others — that the version delivered to the Wedding Guest, for example, in fact improves upon that told to the Hermit. What we do know is that the Mariner must tell his tale over and over. In a like way the text of the poem passes through a series of revisions, with every indication that the revisionary process might have continued endlessly like the Mariner's wanderings. And the compulsive revisions of this text, like the Mariner's own compulsion to tell his tale, indicate not an ultimate closure or completion in a final form, but a shifting, restless re-enactment of events.

By including all the changes from 1798 through 1828, the present edition hopes to lay bare the reflection of the Mariner's compulsion in Coleridge's and how it shapes the text. Every effort has been made to allow no one version to gain priority over any other. Value judgments that determine a given set of changes to be improvements over another set have been suspended. The text may make for difficult reading because it forces the reader into a continual confrontation with the anxieties which are very much a thematic concern of the poem. This edition makes plain that the reasons for the revisions can no longer be found in the desire to improve or to clarify the poem. Thus the "Dutch attempt at German sublimity" of 1798 becomes no less obscure and no less Gothic with the changes in spelling in 1800 or the deletion in 1817 of stanzas dealing with the purple and green mold growing on the skeleton's bones. The gloss does not explain, but only adds another revision.

Read as a continual self-revision, "The Ancient Mariner" extends beyond any one text of determinate meaning into something much less certain. The poem acquires a radically new shape, and places new demands on its readers. The narration no longer confines itself to the Mariner telling the Wedding Guest his tale one time, but rather it expands indefinitely as the poem re-enacts itself through revision. Viewed as the ensemble of revisions in which the poem actually embodies continual re-enactment, the narration now unfolds in a changing context, one less susceptible to a determinate meaning. This is a context created by a text altering itself even to the point of self-contradiction. Indeed, it quickly strikes most readers that the poem consists of two texts in one — the verse and the gloss. The present edition shows how this split does little to clarify the verse narration, instead adding another competing version to the already heavily overladen text. The shifting text here disclosed reveals the Mariner's basic ontological instability. Far from indicating some definite relation between the Mariner and his experience and between the Mariner and his auditor, this text changes in so many details that virtually no relations remain unquestioned.

A powerful compulsion for self-revision is ultimately intrinsic to the nature of "The Ancient Mariner" as text and as narrative. When we no longer view the revisions as developments, our understanding of the poem changes, both in regard to any single version and in regard to the poem as represented in this edition. The poem can no longer be seen as the slow evolution from youthful unpolished enthusiasm to mature judgement and perfection, for each of the seven versions possesses as much beauty as every other. Later versions do not clarify the poem, or bring it into a more certain form; indeed, as the number of versions adds up, the poem forgoes any claim to a definite form.

Speaking generally, Jerome McGann says of the inevitable variants and revisions which make up the events of any textual history:

> Many persons besides the author are engaged in these events, and the entire process constitutes the life of an important social institution at the center of which is the literary work itself (the "work" being a series of specific "texts," a series of specific acts of production, and the entire process which both of these series constitute). For the textual critic, all phases and aspects of these matters are relevant.[42]

In the case of "The Ancient Mariner," this "social institution" provides a meaningful context in which the revisions occur, but only a limited one. This poem raises the issue of revision as the central theme of its narration, and manifests the Mariner's obsession in the very shape of the text itself.

No longer seeking a whole, or a meaning of the poem which must be protected, we must choose another way to read this text, and we must even reconsider what constitutes a text. As this edition shows, the text made up of revisions ceases to be a stable field of signification and instead becomes a restlessly wavering confluence of counter-references and cross-hatchings.

One very important hermeneutical problem arises in regard to differences between editions. Quite often a later text will actually contradict a statement in an earlier text, so that where the early one says, for example, that something happens ("The strong wind reach'd the ship" 1798:329), the later texts will say that it does not ("The loud wind never reached the Ship" 1800:333; 1828: 321). If we insist that the text holds a certain integrity of its own, we cannot simply claim that 1800 corrected the error of 1798. Instead, we must read the poem in its revisions, so that in 1798 the "wind reach'd the ship," while thereafter it did not reach the ship. Looking beyond any single text to the expansive system constituted by all six, we must allow that few — if any — of the revisions are accidental, and then analyze them as a coherent set of relations. After all, in the above example, to make the change and still maintain the metrical order of the line, Coleridge had to drop the last two words of the line and change the next line entirely:

1798
The strong wind reach'd the ship: it roar'd
And dropp'd down, like a stone!
Beneath the lightening and the moon
The dead men gave a groan. (329-32)

1800
The loud wind never reach<e>d the Ship,
Yet now the Ship mov<e>d on!
Beneath the lightening and the moon
The dead men gave a groan. (333-36)[43]

Such variants as this one force us to see the textual changes in a new light. The series of revisions done from 1800 through 1828 follow a complicated development analogous to the thematic development of the Mariner's narration. As the poem passes through the later editions of *Lyrical Ballads* — those of 1800, 1802, and 1805 — it changes considerably from its first manifestation of 1798. When the poem appears in *Sibylline Leaves*, it has again changed, and in many ways returned toward the form of 1798. The present edition enables us actually to read the revisions apart from any scheme that privileges one set over any other, and to read them as a narrative structure in their own right. Grouping the revisions together discloses a thematic development which re-enacts the supposedly singular narration heard by the wedding guest. The textual history of the revisions, in which no thematic statement remains static, is governed only by the same compulsion driving the Mariner to tell his tale endlessly.

The present edition raises some serious questions about Coleridge's poem, both for the history of Romanticism and for reading in general. Allegorical readings, like Robert Penn Warren's, which confirm a singular moral context, must be reconsidered in light of the shifting context.[44] Since this poem has traditionally been seen as one of the major works in Coleridge's canon as well as that of Romanticism, the present edition compels readers to evaluate anew the alignment of Coleridge's moral and philosophical development along with the meaning of Romanticism. And, since the revisions generate a broader context than that allowed by any single, authoritative text, we must examine a reading process which does not read *into* a text but rather *across* or *between* texts, while extending the limits of textual integrity beyond those restraints imposed by some claim to authorial intention.

The Mariner's Restlessness

First of all, we should determine whether there is any thematic reason for the revisionary restlessness. Is it possible to conceive of a time when the Mariner (or Marinere) did not have to tell his tale? Of course there was such a time. He first must tell his story, he informs the Wedding Guest, in response to the Hermit's question, "What manner man art thou?"[45] In 1798 the Marinere says that upon hearing the question,

Forthwith this frame of mine was wrench'd
 With a woeful agony
Which forc'd me to begin my tale
 And then it left me free.

Since then at an uncertain hour,
 Now oftimes and now fewer,
That anguish comes and makes me tell
 My ghastly aventure. (1798:628-31)

After 1800 the second stanza changes into the following:

Since then, at an uncertain hour,
 That agony returns;
And till my ghastly tale is told,
 This heart within me burns. (1800:587-90)

The Hermit's question provides us with at least the inception of the need to tell and retell the "ghastly aventure." But why it should have such an effect on the Marinere remains to be answered. The Hermit asks his question in response to the Marinere's request to be shrived, but what his response is to the story he hears we do not learn. The Hermit asks his question, perhaps, in order to know why he must shrive this man who has come to shore in such a strange fashion. After the ship sinks, the Marinere floats "Like one that had been seven days drown'd" (1798:599). When the Pilot's boat picks him up "swift as dreams," the Pilot falls "in a fit," and the Pilot's boy becomes hysterical. Then the Marinere exclaims:

And now all in mine own Countrée
 I stood on the firm land!
The Hermit stepp'd forth from the boat,
 And scarcely he could stand. (1798:616-19)

All the details associated here with the Marinere, the simile of dreams, the reactions of the Pilot and his boy, and the Hermit's uncertainty, underscore the Marinere's uncanniness. The question that the Hermit asks, then, is directed not merely at hearing confession, but at demanding, requiring, that the Marinere identify himself.

The Hermit's question begins the physical compulsion in the Marinere to tell his tale endlessly. Both the retelling and the physical nature of the compulsion are important. The Marinere has gotten caught up in the impossible task of defining himself. It is impossible because it is endless: he cannot determine the boundaries to his being that would allow him to lay claim to a kind of identity (just as we cannot set the boundaries to a text that would indicate authorial intention). The physical compulsion shows that the question of his identity concerns not some abstract quality, but the Marinere's most fundamental being. He says, "this frame of mine was wrench'd," as though the agony goes beyond his body and extends throughout his entire sense of physical being. The frame is the physical space in which he must find his being and understand it in relation to the world around him: he is framed not only through his active involvement in the world around him, but literally in the text of his tale. But his being cannot be defined, and so he must tell the tale endlessly, precluding definition in every forced attempt.

The Hermit's question compels the Marinere to tell the story that should indicate either what his identity is or why he lacks one. At one level, the story revolves around the central event, the Marinere's killing of the albatross. Even though this event is referred to directly or indirectly elsewhere in the poem, and even though the gloss states explicitly that the Marinere is doing penance, still the greater problem of the event appears to lie in the difficulty the marineres all have of understanding its significance. At first they claim the albatross "made the Breeze to blow" (1798:92), but as soon as events appear to improve, or rather, as soon as the fog dissipates, the marineres reverse their opinion to say it is right to kill birds who bring the fog and mist.

In order to understand what the act of killing the albatross means, the crew try to determine the immediate connection between bird and external events, primarily the weather. Always the men connect the albatross to the nearest contiguous event. When the bird first appears, the ice opens and "a good south wind sprung up behind" (1798:85). The men assume the albatross is what "made the Breeze to blow" (1798:92). When the bird is dead, and the fog clears, they claim that it had been the cause of that malady instead. Then, when the ship bursts into the silent sea and the wind drops, the crew hang the albatross from the Marinere's neck. Thereafter a series of events takes place whose connection never becomes certain; in fact, what proves most disturbing about such scenes as that of the spectre-ship is that they invalidate the very connections on which meaning depends. When the Marinere first sights the "something in the Sky" which becomes "a shape," he calls out "a sail! a sail!" expecting to be saved by a ship (1798:139, 144, 153). What appears instead violates his just expectation that he had based on the synecdochal union of sail and ship. It is indeed a ship that sails up, but not one that meets his understanding of what a ship is or should be. This is a ship that barely exists, whose crew consists of two beings who do not belong in life but in death and in nightmares and who are engaged in a portentous dice game. Again, after the spectre-ship shoots off, the Marinere's crew make another interpretation as they turn their faces to the Marinere and curse him as each dies.[46]

At this point the Marinere himself must struggle for the connections between events and objects. Like the crew, he finds a link between events and the killing of the albatross. And, like the crew, he remains unsure of exactly what that connection is or means. His uncertainty remains the controlling factor throughout his narration and throughout his compulsive retelling. All the subsequent events violate whatever meaningful connections might be expected and offer only nebulous connections in exchange.

The image of the silent sea prevails along with that of the spectre-ship and the albatross to signify the breakdown in signification. The ship and crew "were the first that ever burst / Into that silent Sea" (1798:101-02). Allegorically, they move from the world of meaningful connection to a silence where the connections on which meaning depends are no longer tenable. The silent sea is empty space, and as such simply cannot uphold the relations of meaning or language. The spectre-ship, one of the most disturbing images in romantic literature, acts specifically to destroy the most fundamental boundary, that between life and death. The woman on the spectre-ship remains unnamed until 1817, when she is called LIFE-IN-DEATH (1817:193). Before that time she merely appears couched in a description parodying the traditional ballad account of the bonny young lass:

Her lips are red, *her* looks are free,
   Her locks are yellow as gold:
Her skin is as white as leprosy,
And she is far liker Death than he;
   Her Flesh makes the still air cold. (1798:196-200)

Until we see that her skin is like leprosy, we might take her not for the creature of a spectre-ship, but for a country maid. The closest we get to an actual identification here (and through 1805) is the comparison that "she is far liker Death than he." He, of course, is a "fleshless Pheere," in 1798, which provides us no reference whatsoever to determine her or his relative resemblance to Death. In 1800 he becomes "her Mate" (1800:181) and then "Death" in 1817 (1817:188), even though she had been said to be "far liker Death than he" (1798:199; 1800:190). So, even when he acquires his specific identity of "Death," the woman is already closer to it than he is. And Death can only ever be defined in terms of what it is not — the living. The boundary between the states of life and death is vital to any definition of either state. So, in 1817, when the poem finally identifies the woman with the tantalizingly vague title, "The Night-Mair LIFE-IN-DEATH," it does anything but say who or what she is (1817:193).

The point, however, is that she is no one being. In fact, she does not even represent a being, as such. Her appearance on this ship, which is not a ship, violates the Marinere's expectations. The ship itself violates his expectation of a meaningful connection between the signifying sail and a signified ship, and the woman violates his expectation of a woman, which he expresses in formulaic descriptions. Further, she violates his expectation of a human, who should be either alive or dead, and not both. Her appearance destroys the categorical relations with which the Marinere had already been struggling since killing the albatross and which he would like to maintain as a legitimate system of knowing.

Here in the empty space of the silent sea, the Marinere finds that relations between beings determine their relative identities, and that those relations depend on classification and division into categories. If these categories are violated, if their boundaries are destroyed, the identities of individuals collapse into indeterminacy. The woman confronts the Marinere directly with the indeterminacy

overthrowing categories and thereby identity. His encounter follows this se-
quence: she seems to be a woman, but cannot be because she is dead, but is not
actually dead because she remains active, though not productively so. She is not
alive, is not dead. She is neither a woman, nor a non-woman. All that is left is to
say she is a "Night-Mair," a bad dream that will not go away.

The remainder of the story struggles with the question: to what extent is the
Marinere alone? The narration vacillates, now asserting that he is completely
isolated, now suggesting that perhaps he is not without company. On the one hand,
he is "Alone, alone, all all alone / Alone on the wide wide Sea" (1798:235-36). On
the other hand, "a million million slimy things / Liv'd on — and so did I" (1798:240-
41). If we follow the host of commentators who focus on the Marinere's relation
to the slimy things, we can say that he simply re-affirms his spiritual relation to the
world around him, which he had ignored when he shot the albatross.[47] But if we
recognize that the poem does vacillate on this issue, and if we see how the
vacillation comes out of the earlier failed interpretations, then we see a much more
complex issue than the ultimate affirmation of a tired morality.

The argument that the Marinere re-affirms his spiritual bond to the world
depends on the identification of the "million million slimy things" with the water
snakes. Except for the statements by the gloss calling both the slimy things and the
water snakes "creatures of the calm," there is no clear indication that they are the
same animals. Even if they are the same, however, the Marinere changes his
judgement of them, just as the crew had changed theirs concerning the albatross.
In the first instance he uses them to describe his agony of living among the corpses
of the crew:

> The many men so beautiful,
>   And they all dead did lie!
> And a million million slimy things
>   Liv'd on — and so did I. (1798:238-41)

In the second instance, they are no longer slimy but clad in a "rich attire" of "elfish
light" and "golden fire" (1798:280, 277, 283). Regardless of what moral value we
assign to the Marinere's change of attitude, it nonetheless adds to the general

instability of knowledge: throughout the entire poem, statements of known fact are shown to be merely subjective interpretations, from the Marinere's androcentric descriptions of events ("The Sun came up upon the left, / Out of the Sea came he" [1798:30-31]), to the crew's disastrous interpretations of the albatross, to the slimy water snakes. And after the breakdown of signifying relations in the spectre-ship episode, no clear connection can be upheld between the "slimy things" and "the water-snakes."

From this point in the narration, the questioning of relations turns onto the Marinere himself: the issue of what relation he holds to himself as interpreter of his own being (and, ultimately, as respondent to the Hermit's question) pervades the remainder of the tale. In Part V, after the Marinere sleeps, he never seems quite to awake. While sleeping he dreams the buckets on deck have been filled: "And when I awoke it rain'd . . . . Sure I had drunken in my dreams / And still my body drank" (1798:300-06). A few lines later he says,

> I mov'd and could not feel my limbs,
> I was so light, almost
> I thought that I had died in sleep,
> And was a blessed Ghost. (1798:308-11)

The implied simile of dying in sleep and awakening to ghostliness proves to be more than a mere rhetorical device. This section proceeds to list several miraculous events, all of which occur in violation of the distinction between actuality and dream, living reality and death. The night-mair of destroyed boundaries will not leave him.

The wind, which does not blow but only shakes the sails through its sound, reaches the ship (but only in 1798). The dead men arise to work: "It had been strange, even in a dream / To have seen those dead men rise" (1798:335-06). Like the spectre-ship and its crew, the Marinere's ship and crew violate the boundary which keeps waking reality separate from dream and death. Sleep and dreams become the dominant theme of Part V, as it opens on the Marinere sleeping and dreaming of rain, and it closes on him fallen in a "swound."

In addition to the question posed by the collapse of reality into sleep, this part is filled with the sound which was entirely absent from the previous section. The wind roars far off, so that "with its sound it shook the sails" (1798:314). Though the re-animated corpses do not speak, and the Marinere himself "quak'd" at the thought of his own voice, in the light of day, when the bodies stop working, "Sweet sounds rose slowly thro' their mouths / And from their bodies pass'd" (1798:350-51). The sounds intermingle until they "fill the sea and air / With their sweet jargoning" (1798:359-60). Even when these disembodied sounds cease,

> yet still the sails made on
> A pleasant noise till noon,
> A noise like of a hidden brook
> In the leafy month of June,
> That to the sleeping woods all night
> Singeth a quiet tune. (1798:365-70)

Again we get the conflation in a simile of sleep and "pleasant noise," a noise pleasant because it is hidden and does not pose the directly confrontational threat of the spectre-ship.

The bodies silently work while the ship is carried along by the spirit, "Under the keel nine fathom deep / From the land of mist and snow" (1798:387-88). When the Marinere falls into the swound, he again hears sounds, this time the two voices telling of the death of the albatross and of the spirit under the keel. These disembodied voices contrast with the unvoiced bodies who worked the ship. They also provide the transition from the varied sounds and dreams of Part V to the homecoming of Part VI.

The homecoming is made possible by the silent and motionless wind (it "ne sound ne motion made" [1798:463]). This same wind which has carried the Marinere so far and in such a miraculous way now imposes its character on his homecoming. The wind, he says, "mingled strangely with my fears, / Yet it felt like a welcoming" (1798:467-68). He has come home, and to the same place he has left, but his welcoming is strangely frightening. The very place that is most familiar is at the same time odd. This double quality comes from the violation of boundaries in the earlier sections, and manifests itself now and hereafter as the uncanny — the dual sensation of familiarity and strangeness, which shatters the assumed relations of identity.

It is worth recalling Wordsworth's statement that the plan for a ballad which he and Coleridge concocted was "founded on a dream, as Mr Coleridge said of his friend Cruikshank."[48] The commonest objects appear to the Marinere as in a dream. The night-mair from the silent sea has stayed with him to trouble the mundane comfort of home.[49] Coleridge explains in his notebooks precisely what constitutes the night-mair state:

> Night-mair is, I think, always — even when it occurs in the midst of Sleep, and not as it more commonly does after a waking Interval, a state not of Sleep but of Stupor of the outward organs of Sense, not in words indeed but yet in fact distinguishable from the suspended power of the senses in true Sleep; while the volitions of *Reason* i.e. comparing &c, are awake, tho' disturbed.... In short, this Night-mair is not properly *a Dream*; but a species of Reverie, akin to Somnambulanceism, during which the Understanding & Moral Sense are awake tho' more or less confused, and over the Terrors of which the Reason can exert no influence that because it is not true Terror: i.e. apprehension of Danger, but a sensation as much as the Tooth-ache, a Cramp — I.e. the Terror does not *arise* out of the a painful Sensation, but is itself a specific sensation = terror corporeus sive materialis.[50]

Since his experience on the silent sea, the Marinere has not been able to awake from this "species of Reverie."[51] Not only have "the necessary connections" of understanding dissolved, but so have the distinctions — especially those between states of waking and dreaming — from which the rational reality constructs its moral order.

When the breeze, which blows on the Marinere alone, carries him across the harbor bar, he exclaims, "O dream of joy!" (1798:473). He sees "The light-house top ... the Hill ... the Kirk," and prays, "O let me be awake, my God! / Or let me sleep alway" (1798:474-75; 480-81). Everything he encounters seems comfort-

ingly mundane: the harbour-bay, the moonlight. But from the moonlight arise
"Full many shapes, that shadows were" (1798:487). In 1798 the bodies arise twice
within a few stanzas — once as the "dead-man's hand" torches (1798:490-511), and
again as each "A man all light, a seraph man" (1798:518-37). These lights, the
"seraph band," signal to the shore, but:

> No voice did they impart —
> No voice; but O! the silence sank,
> Like music on my heart. (1798:529-31)

The 1798 version emphasizes the double valence of this event and consequently
the danger of settling on a final interpretation. The bodies might signal either evil
or good. Likewise, it is a joyous homecoming for the Marinere, while at the same
time it is no less harrowing than his experience on the silent sea.

The uncanny silence the Marinere carries along with him makes his home now
a strange place. The moral he now delivers raises large questions about the story
he has told. It suggests that a moral scheme has been enforced throughout the
narration, when in fact the experiences of which the Marinere tells seem to
undermine the possibility of any such scheme. Following from his nightmarish
narration, the Marinere's concluding moral statements seem to be haunted by the
uncanniness infecting his homecoming. He recounts an experience that destroys
the common understanding of experience in general; he tells of his confrontation
with what had remained concealed, but his story shows that direct confrontation
does not disclose everything. From his experience the boundary between the
waking world and dream is dissolved.[52] The uncanniness surrounding the conclud-
ing morality emanates from the dream that has become reality. But this dream-
reality invalidates the formal relations between objects in the world, as well as
those between perceiver and perceived, through which he might have constructed
a safely subjective world.

The persistence of the Marinere's night-mair is most evident in his return home.
His relation to his "own Countrée" (1798:616), poignantly has changed com-
pletely, and so have the two principal terms — he and it — in that relation. Home has

become *un-heimlich*. Just when the Marinere believes he stands "on the firm land," the Hermit asks the question that wrenches his frame (1798:623). Here he learns that home provides him with no more grounds for certainty than did the silent sea.

The Hermit's question, simple as it is, forces the Marinere to confront the terrifying uncertainty that lurks within such a cultural artifact as identity — his own as well as that of his narration. His restlessness comes out of his recognition that the "firm land" is but an echo of what might never have been in the first place. He cannot state this fact directly, however, any more than he can name himself. Having told and even retold his story, the Marinere still cannot provide the final statement that will indicate its significance, as he can provide no principle ordering all the events of his tale, or even any one event. He is still in the same situation he was in when the ship's crew could not decide how to interpret the killing of the albatross. The statement that would put everything in order, of course, is the one that would answer the Hermit's question directly — the statement that would identify the Mariner(e), to say just what "manner man" he is (1798:623). The trouble lies in the form of identification sought by the Hermit's question. Coming at the end of the Marinere's narration to the Wedding Guest, the question follows the form of the statement opening the poem, "It is an Ancyent Marinere" (1798: 1). Framing his own opening statement as an echo to this line, the Marinere says, "there was a ship" (1798:9). The spectre-ship and the ensuing events turn the opening easy expressions of factual ontology into uneasy questions. "It is an Ancyent Marinere" is a statement that teases us as a response to the Hermit's question. The use of the verb "to be" poses the problem since, in the form the Hermit uses, it twists on those divisions that the Marinere has found no longer hold. He cannot say what he is, because any statement would carry too many echoes of other possibilities.

What we can see, when all the different versions of the poem are laid over one another, is that any construct based on the Mariner(e)'s tale is too hazy to hold as an identity. He cannot distinguish himself or provide any boundary to himself. For this reason his tale must go on and on, expanding into contradiction. His inability to name himself opens the text to an instability. The well-wrought object that aesthetic judgement desires, here shifts and wavers. The Marinere's text must continually re-enact itself, as the Marinere must continually re-approach the Hermit's question only to find he still has not answered it.

A Reading of the Revisions

Now we should take up the question of just how different the versions are from one another. If the differences among the six versions could be subordinated to one specific aim not directly implicated in revision, and if that aim became more or less distinct through the revisionary process, then we could say that the underlying purpose of this or any revisionary process is simply correction, and that there is no peculiar problem in this poem which drives it to revision. Any claim that a single aim directs all the revisions can only take the form of an argument for authorial intention. On the other hand, even if the different versions do not move toward the greater clarity of a single aim, the revisions themselves — what is deleted, what is replaced — might indicate another narrative context, what McGann describes as an author's response to "his immediate literary environment."[53] A study of this context would focus on one or more sets of responses that Coleridge made to a given environment. It might focus on his response to the charges of obscurity.[54] It might focus on one aspect of his opium addiction, or his changing religious and philosophical views.[55] The reading I wish to offer, however, turns away from even this historical or biographical context, to take up an interpretive or narrative context at the level of the shifting text. This context originates in the theme of the Mariner's compulsive re-telling of his tale, and is in accord with what we have already seen at work in the Mariner's basic narration. What I hope to show is that the present edition reveals significant differences among the versions, that the text demands we recognize these differences, and that the differences generate a narrative context not confined to, nor available from, any single version.

This edition makes the demand for an uncommon type of reading, one which reads the changes of detail as signifying changes in reference. Such a reading is uncommon in that it would give full weight to those "accidental" details that are commonly overlooked, presumably in the interest of consistency of meaning. Like "The Ancient Mariner," any interpretation of the poem, or of the revisions, must open itself to the likelihood of its own revision. It is very likely that new annotations, new emendations, new notebook passages will crop up here and there. What these will show is that no edition of this poem can ever be complete, any more than the Mariner can ever terminate his repetition. "The Ancient Mariner" opens itself to a multitude of interpretations, and for this reason can be said to disclose problems of interpretation in general. Many literary texts have been revised, but no other series of revisions operates under the same obsessiveness thematized by the narration. The connection between the Mariner's wrenching need to tell his story repeatedly and the text's own need to revise itself repeatedly cannot be forgotten. Much of the Mariner's experience centers around apparently innocuous details — a random sea-bird for instance — just as the revisions often revolve around small textual details. Such slight alterations among details reverberate in both cases throughout the text to extend the Mariner's troubling experience beyond any one account and into a text no more identifiable than the Mariner himself.

From *Lyrical Ballads* to *Sibylline Leaves*

In the summer of 1800, when Coleridge and Dorothy Wordsworth transcribed the poems for the second edition of *Lyrical Ballads*, they made both extensive and striking changes. The first noticeable change is in the placement of the poems: Coleridge's poem has moved from the initial position in the single-volume 1798 *Lyrical Ballads* to the rear of the first volume. As we have seen, the reason for this change lies in Wordsworth's appropriation of *Lyrical Ballads* as his work, with some space allowed for poems "written by a friend" (*EY* 304). "The Ancient Mariner" retained this same position through the next two editions of *Lyrical Ballads* — those of 1802 and 1805.

In the text itself, the first and most obvious revisions occur in the title and the spelling of certain words throughout the poem. Just as the *Lyrical Ballads* changes its basic shape through the change of ownership (it is no longer an anonymous work but William Wordsworth's), so in a parallel fashion, the Rime which had belonged to The Ancyent Marinere changes shape and ownership. It becomes "A Poet's Reverie," anonymous, as though to counter Wordsworth's appropriation of the anonymous 1798 edition. The Marinere has in effect disappeared into an intangible primordiality, represented by The Ancient Mariner, who is now but "A Reverie."

The new title also carries an important ambiguity concerning what the reverie is. It might be the Mariner himself, as the title actually seems to indicate, or it might be the Ancient Mariner's narration. This ambiguity points to the overwhelming problem instigated by the Hermit's question: who is the Mariner? Or, more appropriately, what is the Mariner? The answer, this new title suggests, might be found in the poem: the Mariner *is* the narration which *is* a reverie. The Mariner is a reverie that can never attain a definite form. And, as a reverie, he proceeds to tell a tale about his restless encounter with dreams. This new title underscores the difficulty the Mariner has in determining his relation to himself, for such a relation becomes even more tenuous as he is made into a reverie.

As Campbell points out, Coleridge erased the subtitle from the heading for the 1802 edition, though not from the half-title page.[56] In 1817 the title changes again to "The Rime of The Ancient Mariner," appearing to revert to the original form, but in truth an echo of 1798: the Mariner never recovers from his passage through the Poet's Reverie, which literally alters the shape of his orthographical being from the Ancyent Marinere to the Ancient Mariner.

The changes indicated by the title and spelling extend throughout the poem, and are recognizable in part by the alteration in the Mariner's relation to his narration. In 1805 quotation marks suddenly appear around the Mariner's opening statement to the Wedding Guest. In 1798 the significant stanzas appear thus:

> But still he holds the wedding-guest —
> There was a Ship, quoth he —
> "Nay, if thou'st got a laughsome tale,
> "Marinere! come with me."
>
> He holds him with his skinny hand,
> Quoth he, there was a Ship —
> "Now get thee hence, thou grey-beard Loon!
> "Or my Staff shall make thee skip. (1798:9-16)

In 1805 the Mariner's exclamations are set off with quotation marks just as the

Wedding Guest's have been:

>   But still he holds the wedding<->guest —
>   <">There was a Ship,<"> quoth he —
>   "Nay, if thou'st got a laughsome tale,
>   (")Mariner! come with me."
>
>   He holds him with his skinny hand,
>   Quoth he, <">There was a Ship — <">
>   "Now get thee hence, thou gray-beard Loon!
>   (")Or my Staff shall make thee skip.<"> (1800:9-16)

In 1817 the first of these stanzas is absent, but the Mariner's exclamation remains demarcated:

>   He holds him with his skinny hand,
>   "There was a ship," quoth he,
>   "Hold off! unhand me, grey-beard loon!"
>   Eftsoons his hand dropt he. (1817:8-11)

As the passage through the reverie effects the Mariner's orthographical change, so it determines that his words remain a quotation enclosed within a narration not entirely his own.

In 1805 each time the Mariner begins to speak, his words are separated from the narrator's and from the Wedding Guest's with quotation marks. This same separation continues throughout the 1805 edition. Now, the Wedding Guest's words are consistently enclosed within quotation marks from 1798 on, though quite often in 1798 his words are thus separated at the beginning of his statement, but never closed at the ending.[57]

This blurring of the boundaries of dialogue raises the question of who is speaking when — the narrator who introduces the poem, the Mariner, or the Wedding Guest. Each speaker overlaps the other, dissolving the lines of character, until these boundaries are reinstated in 1805 through the closing effect of the quotation marks. The addition of the quotation marks clearly follows from the change in title in 1800.

As the new title transfers the poem from the Ancyent Marinere to the unnamed poet, the Marinere is reduced from the status of implied narrator embodied by his Rime to that of merely another character in the narration. His speeches are blocked off to show their subordinate status: they belong in the poem and to the poem that is no longer his or identifiable with him.

The fact that the quotation marks appear in 1805 rather than 1800 indicates the cumulative effect of three editions of *Lyrical Ballads* with Wordsworth's name on the title page. The 1805 edition went to press while Coleridge was in Malta.[58] As the collection of poems becomes more identified with Wordsworth, the Rime becomes less identified with the Mariner and the text moves increasingly away from its identification with the 1798 Marinere. The unnamed poet appropriates the text from the Mariner, and must indicate where the text *represents* the Mariner's speech, as the poem has become a poet's reverie of the Ancient Mariner, rather than the Mariner's own rime. Prior to 1805 the quotation marks signify an interruption of the Mariner's narration, that he is quoting another speaker, namely the Wedding Guest. In 1805 the Mariner himself becomes the quotation within another's tale.

The 1817 text retains the quotation marks introducing the Mariner's speech after the Wedding Guest sits on the stone:

> *1805*
> <">The Ship was cheer<e>d, the Harbour clear<e>d —

> *1817*
> |"|The Ship was cheered, the harbour cleared

These quotation marks are not closed, however, at the corresponding point nine lines later where the 1805 text adds quotation marks:

> *1805*
> Higher and higher every day,
>   Till over the mast at noon — <">
> The wedding-guest here beat his breast,
>   For he heard the loud bassoon. (34-37)

1817
Higher and higher every day,
Till over the mast at noon —
The Wedding-Guest here beat his breast,
For he heard the loud bassoon. (29-32)

Nor does the 1817 text use quotation marks to designate the opening of the Mariner's speech hereafter in the poem. In 1828 the quotation marks disappear, so that the speeches return to the form they had prior to 1805. With the attempted return to the first title, the 1817 and 1828 texts effectively give his speech back to the Mariner. We must recall, however, that they give it back to the Mariner rather than to the Marinere.

The addition of quotation marks in the later editions of *Lyrical Ballads* corresponds to the appropriation of those editions by Wordsworth. The extent to which Wordsworth influenced the textual appearance of at least the 1805 "Ancient Mariner" can be surmised from the fact that many changes made in 1805 disappear in 1817. At any rate his appropriation raises serious doubts about the possibility of establishing "authorial intention" for "The Ancient Mariner."[59] The relation between Coleridge and Wordsworth is very complex owing to the intensity of their friendship and collaborations. So many of their great poems echo one another that it is often impossible to demarcate one author from the other during the years of their intimacy.[60]

The larger revisions in "The Ancient Mariner" reflect the same issues raised by the quotation marks. In 1800 ten stanzas are deleted from the poem, while two are added. The deletions occur in the second half of the poem, the additions mostly in the first half. The stanzas dropped are from two scenes in Part V; in the first, the Marinere interrupts his story to tell the Wedding Guest to listen:

Listen, O listen, thou Wedding-guest!
  "Marinere! thou hast thy will:
"For that, which comes out of thine eye, doth make
  "My body and soul to be still."
Never sadder tale was told

> To a man of woman born:
> Sadder and wiser thou wedding-guest!
> Thou'lt rise to morrow morn.
>
> Never sadder tale was heard
>   By a man of woman born:
> The Marineres all return'd to work
>   As silent as beforne.
>
> The Marineres all 'gan pull the ropes,
>   But look at me they n'old:
> Thought I, I am as thin as air—
>   They cannot me behold. (1798:371-86)

The four stanzas deleted here correspond to the one added in 1800 to the scene of the bodies beginning to work the ropes. In 1798 the passage consists of one stanza:

> The body of my brother's son
>   Stood by me knee to knee:
> The body and I pull'd at one rope,
>   But he said nought to me—
> And I quak'd to think of my own voice
>   How frightful it would be! (1798:343-47)

In 1800 the final two lines are dropped, and in 1805 quotation marks close off the Mariner's statement:

> The body of my brother's son
>   Stood by me knee to knee:
> The body and I pull<e>d at one rope,
>   But he said nought to me.<">
> "I fear thee, ancient Mariner![”]
>   <">Be calm, thou \W\edding<->\G\uest!

> 'Twas not those souls[,] that fled in pain,
>   Which to their corses came again,
> But a troop of Spirits blest: (1800:346-54)

The Wedding Guest fears the implications of the Mariner sharing a ship with animated corpses. The Mariner calms him, oddly, with the clarification that he was not standing among painfully departed souls but "a troop of Spirits blest" who had not been previously associated with the men.

This group of revisions shifts the interruption from the Marinere to the Wedding Guest. In 1798 the Marinere quakes at the thought of his own voice, and then, as though still painfully aware of his "strange power of speech," implores the Wedding Guest to listen to this saddest of tales. In 1800 the anxiety shifts away from the Mariner to the Wedding Guest. Indeed, the Mariner continues his narration as though explaining further why the Wedding Guest should stay calm: "For when it dawn<e>d—they dropp<e>d their arms" (1800:355). In 1798, when the Marinere tells of quaking at his own voice, he says more abruptly, "The day-light dawn'd—they dropp'd their arms" (1798:349). In the earlier text the events of dawn do not prove the existence of a benign force, but constitute only another inexplicable episode. The comfort afforded in 1800 hearkens back to the crew's attempts to interpret the significance of the albatross and its death. In his earlier manifestation, the Marinere's "own voice" disturbs him. In 1800 not only is he no longer so disturbed, but he calms his auditor's fears. But the 1800 Mariner, we recall, has lain off speaking in his own voice, since he has been appropriated by the anonymous poet.[61]

Sometime after the 1805 edition, Coleridge reworked a stanza in his notebook. This passage deserves special consideration because it received so much attention from Coleridge, who returned to it repeatedly from about 1806 through 1828. In the four editions of *Lyrical Ballads* the passage consists of two stanzas:

> With never a whisper in the Sea
>   Off darts the Spectre-ship;
> While clombe above the Eastern bar
> The horned Moon, with one bright star

> Almost atween the tips.
>
> One after one by the horned Moon
>   (Listen, O Stranger! to me)
> Each turn'd his face with a ghastly pang
>   And curs'd me with his ee. (1798:209-18)

The notebook entry blurs the division of two stanzas:

> With never a whisper on the main
>   Off shot the spectre-ship;
> And stifled words & groans of pain
>   murmuring
>   Mix'd on each ~~trembling~~ lip/
> And/we look'd round, & we look'd up,
> And fear at our hearts, as at a cup,
> The Life-blood seem'd to sip —
> The sky was dull, & dark the night,
> The Helmsman's Face by his lamp gleam'd bright,
>   From the sails the Dews did drip/
>   clombe
> Till ~~rose~~ above the Eastern Bar,
> The horned Moon, with one bright star
>   Within its nether Tip. (1800:205-16)

Kathleen Coburn dates this entry quite precisely as 5-12 October 1806, suggesting connections both to the Longman offer of a two-volume edition of Coleridge's poetry and to the Malta trip.[62] In *Sibylline Leaves* the passage appears without a gloss:

> The Sun's rim dips; the stars rush out:
> At one stride comes the dark;
> With far-heard whisper, o'er the sea,

Off shot the spectre-bark.

We listen'd and look'd sideways up!
Fear at my heart, as at a cup,
My life-blood seemed to sip!
The stars were dim, and thick the night,
The steersman's face by his lamp gleamed white;

From the sails the dews did drip—
Till clombe above the eastern bar
The horned Moon, with one bright star
Within the nether tip.

One after one, by the star-dogged Moon,
Too quick for groan or sigh
Each turned his face with a ghastly pang,
And curs'd me with his eye. (1817:205-19)

The development of this passage is clearly complex. Confining our reading to the text, and not to Coleridge's observations during his voyage to Malta, we can see that the evolution here follows the same course we have seen elsewhere. The overall effect of adding these stanzas is to enhance the terror of the spectre-ship. Previously, in all editions of *Lyrical Ballads*, the spectre-ship darts off and the crew curse the Mariner, then die, while the Mariner only interrupts parenthetically to insist that the Wedding Guest pay attention. The added stanzas curiously no longer require the interruption.

What distinguishes the 1806 notebook entry from either the earlier *Lyrical Ballads* or the later *Sibylline Leaves* version is the inclusion of the crew in the description of terror. In this version, "stifled words & groans of pain / Mix'd on each [murmuring] lip" (1800:207-08). In stark contrast to their earlier willingness to decide the meaning of the albatross and its death, here the crew cannot speak, for "fear at our hearts, as at a cup, / The Life-blood seem'd to sip" (1800:210-11).[63]

This passage, and Coleridge's attention to it, suggest that the spectre-ship, and not the slaughter of the albatross, is the dominant experience the Mariner has on his voyage. The spectre-ship literally stifles any attempt at interpretation. What it *might* mean is so terrible that the men feel their life-blood sipped away by fear. What it does mean simply cannot be said, since it violates all categories of meaning.

In *Sibylline Leaves* the spectre-ship shoots off "With far-heard whisper" (1817:205). The men do not comment, but the noise of the spectre-ship, explicitly absent prior to 1817, gives them something to listen to. The fear belongs exclusively to the Mariner as he looks around him at the gloomy night. As the focus shifts to him, the scene becomes the account of his subjective experience. There is no interpretation, only individual isolation and fear.

Coleridge's interest in this scene also appears in the only extensive revision of any part of the gloss. This comment went through at least five increasingly terse stages, resulting in that particular statement in which Lowes found such joy: "No twilight within the courts of the sun."[64] The gloss seems determined not to comment on the terror, choosing instead to veil the scene in an archaic metaphor. This gloss appears in 1828 and is the only addition Coleridge made to the commentary after 1817.

The Marginal Gloss

In the 1817 edition there first appeared the most famous revision, the marginal gloss. With the gloss the poem takes on an entirely new shape. Ostensibly the title designates a return to the earlier form of the poem, but with the modernized orthography of the Mariner, the poem now splits itself into two contrasting voices.

Kathleen Wheeler fruitfully suggests that the gloss grows out of the two versions of the Argument which existed prior to 1817.[65] Hers is an interesting suggestion in that both Arguments constitute a strongly moralistic view of the poem that is not borne out by any but the weakest aspect of the Mariner's narration — that is, the very end. Likewise, the gloss maintains a very definite moral stand throughout its summary of the poem. And R. C. Bald's account of the annotation of a copy of 1800 *Lyrical Ballads* shows a transitional stage between the argument and the gloss.

Bald quotes Coleridge's annotation which was to have replaced the ultimate clause in the 1800 Argument — "and in what manner he came back to his own Country":

> the Spirit, who loved the Sea-bird pursuing him & his Compan-
> ions, & sh[ ] up against them two Spectres; and ho[w] left alone
> in the becalmed Vessel; ho[w] his guardian Saint took pity on
> him; & [how] a choir of Angels descended, and entered into the
> bodies of the men who died; & and in what manner he ca[me]
> back to his own Country.[66]

(The brackets in Bald's annotation mark the damage done by the binder.) Bald also quotes an annotation which might have developed into the gloss to the stanza where the Wedding Guest interrupts out of fear that the Mariner is one of the reanimated bodies (1800:350):

> By the interception of his kind saint a choir of angels desc[ended]
> from Heaven, & entered into the dead bod[ies] using the bodies
> a[s] material Instrum[ents].[67]

If we accept the argument that the gloss was written during the 1800-1805 period, we can again see the effect of Wordsworth's domination. As Wordsworth laid greater claim to *Lyrical Ballads*, Coleridge pushed the Mariner's narration back into anonymity by changing the title, and working on another narration in a different anonymous voice.[68]

Ultimately though, any claim of origin for the gloss is moot. The gloss arises like the many other changing details of the poem, irreversibly changing the shape of the text. And, just as the other versions are effected by small or large changes, the gloss distinguishes itself in an autonomous form, even though it ostensibly depends on the poem. The commentary the gloss provides is compelling and seductive in its claim to explain the essential meaning of the poem, and yet it imposes an interpretation at odds with much of the Mariner's narration.

The first comment of the gloss which is noticeably distant from the Mariner's narration comes at the climactic ending of Part I, when the Mariner shoots the albatross: "The ancient Mariner inhospitably killeth the pious bird" (1817:80). Up to this point, the gloss has referred to the Mariner four times, calling him "An ancient Mariner" at the opening of the poem, "the old sea faring man" fifteen lines into the poem, and "the Mariner" twice when explaining what the Mariner tells the Wedding Guest. In each of these four instances, the gloss is concerned with the fact that the Mariner is addressing the Wedding Guest, not with the events on the sea. When the gloss identifies "the ancient Mariner" as the one who kills the bird, it blurs the distance between the actual event and the telling of the event. The man who kills the albatross is not necessarily old; only the man who stops the Wedding Guest is. In 1832, regarding some engravings for the poem by David Scott, Coleridge is recorded as stating:

> It is an enormous blunder . . . to represent the Ancient Mariner
> as an old man on board ship. He was in my mind the everlasting
> wandering Jew — had told this story ten thousand times since the
> voyage which was in early youth and fifty years before.[69]

By blurring the distinction between the events told and the telling, the gloss bypasses the problem of identity which troubles the Mariner from the first time he begins to tell his tale.

Furthermore, the gloss imposes its judgement on the quality of events within the Mariner's narration. On the albatross the gloss comments:

> And lo! the Albatross proveth a bird of good omen, and followeth
> the ship as it returned northward through fog and floating ice.
> (1817:71)

At this point the albatross has proved nothing; it simply appears, eats "the food it ne'er had eat," and then follows when "A good south wind sprung up behind" (1817:67, 71). By calling the bird a "good omen," the gloss connects it directly to the wind.

In Part II when the crew cannot decide whether killing the bird holds good or bad significance, the gloss clearly knows. While the crew change their interpre-

tation of the slaughter, the gloss remains consistent. First, the Mariner's account
of the crew's switch in interpretation:

> And I had done a hellish thing,
> And it would work 'em woe:
> For all averred, I had killed the bird
> That made the breeze to blow.
> Ah wretch! said they, the bird to slay,
> That made the breeze to blow!
>
> Nor dim nor red, like God's own head,
> The glorious Sun uprist:
> Then all averred, I had killed the bird
> That brought the fog and mist.
> 'Twas right, said they, such birds to slay,
> That bring the fog and mist. (1817:92-102)

Of this same scene the gloss says:

> His ship-mates cry out against the ancient Mariner, for killing
> the bird of good luck.
>
> But when the fog cleared off, they justify the same, and thus
> make themselves accomplices in the crime.

According to the gloss, because the crew cannot determine the proper relations
between albatross and weather, they become accessories after the fact. The gloss
itself, however, sees consistently meaningful relations among beings in the world
and events. The albatross belongs to the spirit of the land of mist and snow. So,
because the albatross holds direct connections to other beings, for the gloss, its
appearance can effectively signify other appearances, such as that of the "good
south wind." Killing the bird, therefore, clearly violates the regional order by
opening a gap within the system of connections among creatures and among

creatures and events. The gloss can make its moral interpretation only because it maintains a faith in a moral universe. To the gloss, any act that does not celebrate the moral connectedness or that does not reinforce this connectedness violates the moral code and must be punished. Thus, when the crew withdraw their interpretation that the albatross "made the breeze to blow," they become guilty of a crime almost as serious as the Mariner's.

What the gloss shows us is the recoiling of the text onto itself as a self-interpretation. Such interpretation remains necessarily removed from the event itself and is possible only within the ideological framework that removes it from the event. Given the Mariner's tale of dreams and doubtful beings, the gloss's self-assured understanding can only be possible at a considerable remove from the Mariner and his agonized telling and retelling of that tale. The gloss reads the Mariner's text as though it is the only version of the tale. It assumes that the narration is stable and that what is present is trustworthy. So much of the Mariner's harrowing trouble stems from his inability any longer to provide a definite answer to the question of identity. He continually gets caught up in having to interpret the events that supposedly identify him. The distance between what he is and the signifiers of his identity pushes him into an endless series of interpretations. When the poem splits itself into a double text of verse and prose, it shows this distance at work.[70]

Scholarship has obscured the gap between the gloss and the Mariner's narration by accepting the gloss as a clarification. Campbell, for example, makes a noteworthy emendation to the gloss at 1817 line 41. Where Coleridge's gloss reads, "The ship drawn by a storm toward the south pole," Campbell changes it to: "The ship driven by a storm toward the south pole."[71] He comments:

> I have ventured to take the liberty of altering *drawn* into *driven*. As a matter of fact, the ship *was* driven not 'drawn,' along. The line in *Sib. Leaves* reads — 'And *chased* us south along': but in all the four preceding texts it was — 'Like chaff we *drove* along': and the change in the word here makes no change in the sense. Coleridge, I have no doubt, wrote *driven*, but in very small characters on the narrow margin of the *Lyrical Ballads*; the

word was misprinted *drawn*, and the mistake was overlooked
then and after. The two words, written or printed, are not easily
distinguishable.[72]

Garnett, in his edition, concurs, stating, "Mr Dykes Campbell improves upon all
preceding editors by correcting *drawn* into *driven*. He might have fortified his
emendation by referring to the Argument: 'How a ship having passed the line was
driven by storms.'"[73] E. H. Coleridge, in turn, keeps Campbell's change in the 1912
Poetical Works from Oxford, which has remained the definitive edition.

Campbell's emendation assumes that the gloss is not merely interpreting but
guiding us toward the authoritative meaning of the poem. He makes the change on
the basis of consistency, assuming that the gloss is correct in its judgement. Camp-
bell overlooks the distance between the Mariner's narration and the gloss and gives
the gloss priority over the Mariner's text, accepting the gloss as a clarification of
the narration. Lowes also shows himself prejudiced by the gloss's interpretation:
"The gloss is explicit, should the poem leave us blind," he says in reference to the
passage on the journeying moon.[74] Prior to Campbell's change, the gloss revealed
itself again at this point to be relying on a frame of belief not necessarily implicated
in the poem.

When the gloss says, "The ship drawn by a storm toward the south pole," it
anticipates its later discussion of the complex structure of spirits and dæmons
(1817:41). Nothing in the Mariner's account, at this point, justifies the gloss's
interpretation. According to the Mariner:

> And now the STORM-BLAST came, and
> Was tyrannous and strong:
> He struck us with his o'ertaking wings,
> And chased us south along.
>
> With sloping masts and dipping prow,
> As who pursued with yell and blow
> Still treads the shadow of his foe
> And forward bends his head,

> The ship drove fast, loud roar/e/d the blast,
> And southward aye we fled.
>
> And now there came both mist and snow,
> And it grew wondrous cold:
> And ice, mast-high, came floating by,
> As green as emerald. (1817:41-54)

This passage describes everything from a point of view strikingly different from that of the gloss. The Mariner consistently, here and elsewhere, speaks androcentrically: the sun has risen on the left and moved to the right, everything he sees approaches or moves away from him and the ship. The storm-blast comes, and chases the ship. Likewise, at the end of the chase, "both mist and snow" come.

It is important to note that the middle stanza in this passage only appears in 1817, at the same time as the gloss. This stanza strongly emphasizes that the storm does *drive* the ship and men southward as they flee in fright. It casts the weather as a vicious opponent. The point of view of this passage, with the added stanza, is consistent with the Mariner's androcentric account of events. The gloss, on the other hand, considers all events according to their moral significance within its ideological framework. From this perspective the storm clearly acts as agent of the forces who require the Mariner to kill the albatross. The storm, in the neoplatonic scheme, is the parallel to the spirit "nine fathom deep" who drives the ship northward in Part V. Just as the neoplatonic structure upholds the value of the albatross through an assumed intimate (even synecdochic) connection to the guardian spirit, so it places the storm in this same meaningful scheme as an intentional agent guiding the Mariner to his fate. All the events happen so that the Mariner can return home and wander about teaching "by his own example, love and reverence to all things that God made and loveth" (1817:614). The Mariner has his role in this highly structured world and he fulfills it by recounting his tale.

The gloss begins its discussion of the neoplatonic spiritual world around line 131:

> A spirit had followed them; one of the invisible inhabitants of
> this planet, neither departed souls nor angels; concerning whom

the learned Jew, Josephus, and the Platonic Constantinopolitan,
Michael Psellus, may be consulted. They are very numerous and
there is no climate or element without one or more.

Much later, when the dead crew arise to work the ship, the gloss explains:

The bodies of the ship's crew are inspirited and the ship moves
on|.|/;/

But not by the souls of the men, nor by dæmons of earth or middle
air, but by a blessed troop of angelic spirits, sent down by the
invocation of the guardian saint. (1817:331-34, 349-57)

The gloss continues to explain that when the spirit from the land of mist and snow
carries the ship from "nine fathom deep," it acts "in obedience to the angelic
troop|;|/,/ but still requireth vengeance" (1817:381-85). But then,

The Polar Spirit's fellow-dæmons, the invisible inhabitants of
the element, take part in the wrong. (1817:396-405)

While the Polar Spirit has been accorded "penance long and heavy for the Ancient
Mariner," and therefore returns south, the ship continues to move onward, now
propelled by "angelic power" (1817:496).[75]
    The effect of the gloss's account is indeed a clearer explanation of why things
happen as they do. But the Mariner's experience is in continual violation of the
explainable. The gloss's account introduces agents that do not overtly have a place
in the Mariner's understanding — or at least in his account of his understanding. To
the Mariner these events remain inexplicable just as events in dreams are
inexplicable. Indeed, the disturbing quality of the events stems from his inability
to explain them. The gloss's explanation depends on a realm that the Mariner does
not admit. Where the Mariner finds the boundary between dream and waking
reality blurred, the gloss identifies this space as that inhabited by dæmons, spirits,
and angels. By opening this space, the gloss can explain the unexplainable and give
moral meaning to what had overthrown the possibility of meaning and morals. In

opening this realm, however, the gloss closes off the inexplicable quality of the Mariner's tale, and reinstates the possibility of boundaries between realms. Boundaries legitimize experience, but only through classification. The peculiarity of the Mariner's experience lies in its violation of all classification.[76]

The gloss imposes on the Mariner's account a moral hierarchy openly derived from neoplatonic sources, and thus achieves two ends. First, it fills the Mariner's empty space with an organizational complex in which everything possesses inherent meaning within determined boundaries. Second, it interposes a mediary world between itself and the Mariner's frightening narration.

The gloss fills the world with its numerous "invisible inhabitants of this planet" on the authority of "the learned Jew, Josephus, and the Platonic Constantinopolitan, Michael Psellus." With these inhabitants the gloss constructs a narration about events external to the Mariner's own narration. These events conveniently explain some of the more baffling sections of the Mariner's tale. Whereas in the Mariner's account, the spirit from the land of mist and snow had been singly involved with the Mariner, following the ship "nine fathom deep," in the gloss's account the "Guardian Saint" intercedes between the spirit and the Mariner, by introducing the angelic spirits whom the antarctic spirit must obey. The gloss is very specific in identifying these spirits, saying they are neither "dæmons of earth or middle air, but . . . a blessed troop of angelic spirits" (1817:349). The Polar Spirit no longer seeks penance from the Mariner on its own, but is instead "accorded" penance by some higher authority in the hierarchy (1817:405). Everything in this world has its proper place and acts in accord with a higher edict. In such a full world every thing and every event has meaning that the observer can determine simply by specifying the context in which the thing or event occurs. The problem the crew faces of how to interpret the killing of the albatross is therefore never encountered in the world of the gloss.

The mediary world constructed by the gloss allows for a clear understanding of the Mariner's experiences, but it is not the world of the Mariner. The gloss at all levels emphasizes the problems of interpretation, namely that any account of the Mariner's experiences ultimately succumbs to the uncertainty of interpretation. The Mariner cannot overcome the distance between identity and interpretation, and so must tell his tale endlessly. The gloss embodies that distance in the new shape it gives the text, that of the schizoid speaking in two voices at the same time.

The gloss's mediary world depends on its claim to authority. It is this implicit claim that distinguishes the gloss from all other versions of the tale. The tale we see the Mariner narrate undermines any claim to identity, while the explanation offered by the gloss establishes a definite identity for the Mariner as teacher of God's love. In this way the gloss successfully overshadows the Mariner's troubled violation of the very moral structure on which the gloss's own authority depends. When the gloss calls on Josephus and Michael Psellus, it essentially achieves for itself what it aims to achieve for the Mariner, namely, placement within a larger discourse. The gloss points to these neoplatonists as authorities on the existence and activities of "the invisible inhabitants of this planet." In this move the gloss gives its own account a ground in knowledgeable discourse and, by thus showing that this discourse precedes it, the gloss asserts that it also speaks justly and authoritatively.

The role of the gloss is very complicated. My discussion of it attempts to turn from the view that it expresses Coleridge's own understanding of the poem, for this view holds that the gloss clarifies when in fact it obscures the poem under its moralistic framework. In a poem as textually unstable as "The Ancient Mariner," the addition of another version must be seen in the context of the continual addition of versions. The consistency of addition, rather than any single addition, is the dominant characteristic of the poem. Once we place the gloss in the context of revision, on the same level as the other changes made to the poem, it loses its authority and becomes simply another version. From this perspective the gloss gains the new value of forcing the text into a physical manifestation of the endless multiplicity of narrations. In this schizoid shape, the text illustrates the fundamental problem in working toward an individual identity: any narrative account of identity can only *refer* to the identity and thus never actually *be* what it claims.

In asserting its authority over the Mariner's own narration, the gloss makes the verse narration into an artifact which can no longer speak for itself. The narration must be placed within a context that will make it meaningful, despite the fact that the narration makes clear that for the Mariner such contexts no longer support *heimlich* meaning. The gloss shows the danger and the inevitability of interpretation, and that an interpretation — no matter how authoritative — will force the textual artifact into a different ideological context. The gloss also shows how all interpretation, at least of this poem, passes through much the same compulsive re-enactment of the tale as the Mariner does. In this regard all readings of the poem follow the course of re-telling the Mariner's tale.[77] The nature of "The Ancient Mariner" is its compulsion for revision. Like the Wedding-Guest, anyone seized by this poem finds that its power lies in its commanding compulsion.

In the presence of such a compulsive narration as "The Ancient Mariner," any apparent structure opens itself to interpretive readings which turn it into another story. In an edition such as this one which exposes the considerable changes the text underwent over a thirty-year period, the injunction simply to describe the changes is well nigh impossible to satisfy. Even though the Mariner's compulsive narration undermines the claim to meaning through story telling, all our best efforts at historical description soon become little more than new versions of the old story. As we move from observers to narrators, we effectively re-enact the Mariner's situation of having to tell the tale which seems less and less to be his own, while our shifting interpretations feed the compulsion lying at the heart of the whole process. Scholarship becomes increasingly exact in telling the story of its own interpretation, and yet it fervently upholds the ruse that it is not merely telling tales but preserving truths.

Notes

[1] William Wordsworth, *Memoirs of William Wordsworth* (London, 1851) I:107, 108; quoted in James Dykes Campbell, ed., *The Complete Poetical and Dramatic Works of Samuel Taylor Coleridge* (London, 1893) 594.

[2] Campbell 594. "Communicated by the Rev. Alex. Dyce to H.N. Coleridge." See also *The Poems of Samuel Taylor Coleridge*, ed. Derwent and Sara Coleridge (London, 1852) 383-84.

[3] William and Dorothy Wordsworth, *The Letters of William and Dorothy Wordsworth: The Early Years, 1787-1805*, ed. Ernest de Selincourt (Oxford: The Clarendon P, 1967) 211. Hereafter cited as *EY*.

[4] Samuel Taylor Coleridge, *Table Talk*, ed. Carl Woodring, vol. 14 of *The Collected Works of Samuel Taylor Coleridge*, gen. eds. Kathleen Coburn and Bart Winer, 2 vols. (Princeton: Princeton UP, 1990) I:205, and note.

[5] Samuel Taylor Coleridge, *Collected Letters of Samuel Taylor Coleridge*, ed. Earl Leslie Griggs. 6 vols. (Oxford: The Clarendon P, 1956-71) I:357. Hereafter cited as *CL*.

[6] Samuel Taylor Coleridge, *Biographia Literaria*, ed. James Engell and W. Jackson Bate, vol. 7 of *The Collected Works*, 2 vols. (Princeton: Princeton UP, 1983) II:5-8.

[7] John E. Jordan provides a close study of the early project of *Lyrical Ballads* in *Why the Lyrical Ballads? The Background, Writing, and Character of Wordsworth's 1798 Lyrical Ballads* (Berkeley: U of California P, 1976). Jordan argues that "The 'Ancient Mariner' does seem to have been the nucleus around which the *Lyrical Ballads* grew, although probably in a much less systematic fashion than the two authors' later accounts suggest" (13-14). Stephen Maxfield Parrish also studies the collaboration, but from the perspective of a "dyspathy" (*The Art of the Lyrical Ballads* [Cambridge: Harvard UP, 1973] 39). Parrish points out that "As the poets' own critical statements emphasize, poetry took its origin for the one in memory, for the other in fantasy or dream" (41).

[8] Jordan makes the deduction that Wordsworth's eviction from Alfoxden spurred the poets toward publication and the trip to Germany (21, 29-32).

[9] Responding to Southey's hostile review of *Lyrical Ballads*, Wordsworth wrote: "He knew that I published those poems for money and money alone. He

145

knew that money was important to me. If he could not consciously have spoken differently of the volume, he ought to have declined the task of reviewing it" (*EY* 267-68). A. M. Buchan, in "The Influence of Wordsworth on Coleridge," *University of Toronto Quarterly* 32 (1963), argues that Coleridge proposed the partnership, as he had earlier with Lamb and Lloyd, to make some badly needed money (359). Mark L. Reed, in "Wordsworth, Coleridge, and the 'Plan' of the *Lyrical Ballads,*" *University of Toronto Quarterly* 34 (1965): 238-53, shows that, despite Coleridge's claim in *Biographia Literaria*, the "Plan" of publishing poems on two types of subject did not come into being until after all the poems had been written. The significance of this point, as we shall see below, lies in the congealing of Wordsworth's poetic ambition as the result of the poems he wrote at this time.

[10] Campbell xliv.

[11] Campbell xlv.

[12] Jordan 41-52.

[13] The most detailed study of the printing history of *Lyrical Ballads* is that of D. F. Foxon, "The Printing of *Lyrical Ballads,* 1798," *The Library,* 5th series, 9 (1954): 221-41. Also see R. W. Daniel, "The Publication of *Lyrical Ballads,*" *Modern Language Review* 22 (1938): 406-10.

[14] Reprinted in *The Romantics Reviewed: Contemporary Reviews of British Romantic Writers,* ed. Donald H. Reiman. 9 vols. (New York: Garland P, 1972) I:128.

[15] *The Romantics Reviewed* I:309. Southey's review appeared in *Critical Review,* 2nd Series, 24 (October 1798): 197-204.

[16] *The Romantics Reviewed* I:8.

[17] For a complete discussion of the reception of *Lyrical Ballads,* and the relation of the volume to the popular "magazine poems," see Robert Mayo, "The Contemporaneity of the *Lyrical Ballads,*" *PMLA* 69 (1954): 486-522. Also see Jordan 53-154; Jordan's emphasis is on Wordsworth as the one most responsible for *Lyrical Ballads.*

[18] *Table Talk,* ed. Carl Woodring. II:375.

[19] Stephen Gill, *Wordsworth: A Life* (Oxford: The Clarendon P, 1989) 184-85.

[20] *The Prose Works of William Wordsworth,* ed. W. J. B. Owen and Jane Worthington Smyser, 3 vols. (Oxford: The Clarendon P, 1974) I:167. In a letter of 2 October 1800, Wordsworth precisely instructs the printers on the appearance

of the title page and the ordering of the notes to "The Thorn" and "The Ancient
Mariner" *(EY* 303-04).

²¹ Reed 249-50.

²² See W. J. B. Owen's Appendix to his edition of *Lyrical Ballads* (Oxford:
Oxford UP, 1967) 153.

²³ Gill 187.

²⁴ Gill 185.

²⁵ The entire note appended to "Christabel" was to read: "For the sake of variety,
and from a consciousness of my own weakness, I have again requested the
assistance of a friend who contributed largely to the first volume, and who has now
furnished me with the Poem of CHRISTABEL, without which I should not yet have
ventured to present a second volume to the public" (Campbell 602). Richard
Holmes argues that the episode of the 1800 *Lyrical Ballads* and "Christabel" helps
to explain Coleridge's turn from poetry, as Wordsworth's rejection of the poem
effectively meant his rejection of Coleridge as a poet: "Coleridge submitted
himself to Wordsworth in the most humiliating and damaging way; while
Wordsworth had shown extraordinary insensitivity to the effect that this rejection
would have on Coleridge's powers and self-confidence" *(Coleridge: Early
Visions* [New York: Penguin, 1989]) 285-86.

²⁶ *The Notebooks of Samuel Taylor Coleridge,* ed. Kathleen Coburn and Merton
Christensen, 4 vols. to date (Princeton: Princeton UP, 1957−) II:2880; Add MS
47508 f.5, in the British Library.

²⁷ Campbell xxi-xxii.

²⁸ This volume was first published by Biggs and Cottle in 1796, with a second
edition in 1797. The third edition was published by Longman in 1803.

²⁹ R. C. Bald, "The Ancient Mariner," *Times Literary Supplement,* 26 July 1934:
528.

³⁰ John Livingston Lowes, *The Road to Xanadu: A Study in the Ways of the
Imagination* (Boston: Houghton Mifflin, 1927) 476.

³¹ For the publication history concerning primarily *Biographia Literaria,* see
James Engell and W. Jackson Bate, "Editor's Introduction" to *Biographia
Literaria* I:xlv-lxvii.

³² See *Blackwoods Magazine* April 1819: p. 112 for an account of the
bankruptcy.

[33] The fullest discussion of the evolution of the new gloss is that of Lowes, 164-68. See also R. C. Bald, "Coleridge and *The Ancient Mariner*: Addenda to *The Road to Xanadu*," in *Nineteenth Century Studies*, ed. Herbert Davis, William C. DeVane, and R. C. Bald (Ithaca: Cornell UP, 1940) 14-15; and "The Ancient Mariner" *TLS* 528.

[34] Campbell 557.

[35] At least one biographer shapes her study of the poet around the poem, using allusions to the Mariner's story as headings to various periods of Coleridge's life: "Shooting the Albatross," "The Courts of the Sun," "Alone on a Wide Sea." See Molly Lefebure, *Samuel Taylor Coleridge: A Bondage of Opium* (New York: Stein and Day, 1974) 8.

[36] Jerome McGann, "The Meaning of The Ancient Mariner," *Critical Inquiry* 8 (1981):38.

[37] McGann, "The Meaning of The Ancient Mariner" 48.

[38] McGann, "The Meaning of The Ancient Mariner" 57.

[39] McGann provides a detailed and thoughtful commentary on the development of the tradition of authorial intention in *A Critique of Modern Textual Interpretation* (Chicago: U of Chicago P, 1983).

[40] S. T. Coleridge, *Poetical Works*, ed. E. H. Coleridge, 2 vols. (Oxford: Oxford UP, 1912) I:186-209. Other modern editions of the 1798 version of "The Ancient Mariner" are R. L. Brett and A. R. Jones, eds., *Wordsworth and Coleridge, The Lyrical Ballads* (London: Methuen, 1965) 9-35, with notes, 273-78; and W. J. B. Owen, ed., *Wordsworth and Coleridge: Lyrical Ballads, 1798*, 7-32, with commentary, 118-26.

[41] William Empson and David Pirie, eds., *Coleridge's Verse: A Selection* (London: Faber and Faber, 1972) 209, 215.

[42] McGann, *Critique* 52.

[43] B. R. McElderry, Jr. states in regard to the 1798 account of the wind: "It appears that in the first reading Southey simply could not make out whether the wind blew on the ship or not; and neither can anyone else. Certainly this account of the wind is worse than purposeless" ("Coleridge's Revisions of 'The Ancient Mariner,'" *Studies in Philology* 29 [1932]: 74).

[44] Robert Penn Warren, "A Poem of Pure Imagination: An Experiment in Reading," *Selected Essays* (New York: Random House, 1958) 198-305.

[45] This is the form which the Hermit's question takes in 1798. Thereafter he asks, "What manner of man art thou?"

[46] Daniel Stempel focusses on the crew's interpretive difficulty as an expression of Schiller's *Aesthetic Education of Man*: "Coleridge's Magical Realism: A Reading of *The Rime of the Ancient Mariner*," *Mosaic* 12 (1978): 143-56. Lorne Forstner, on the other hand, argues that this scene illustrates an attempt to break away from culturally mediated experiences to encounter reality more freely and fully: "Coleridge's 'The Ancient Mariner' and the Case for Justifiable 'Mythocide': An Argument on Psychological, Epistemological and Formal Grounds," *Criticism* 18 (1976): 211-29.

[47] See, for example, Warren 253-61. H. W. Piper takes this view even further to argue that the Mariner's newly gained sympathy with nature, and the plethora of spirits express Coleridge's conception that "nature is embodied in spirits who are at once intelligent natural forces and divine agents": *The Active Universe: Pantheism and the Concept of Imagination in the English Romantic Poets* (London: The Athlone P, 1962) 98. Piper's argument holds even greater interest as an account of the neoplatonic framework, which Coleridge would have developed in connection with his readings on phlogiston, electricity, and light (99-105).

[48] Wordsworth *Memoirs* 107; Campbell 594.

[49] Coburn points out: "The spelling *Night-mair*, not 'Nightmare,' is not incidental; *mair* is used deliberately by Coleridge, meaning a sister or hag in Chap 18 *Biographia Literaria*" (*CN* III:4046n).

[50] *CN* III:4043. See also the letter to Thomas Poole in 1796, concerning Charles Lloyd's illness: "He falls at once into a kind of Night-mair; and all the Realities round him mingle with, and form a part of, the strange Dream. All his voluntary powers are suspended; but he perceives & hears every thing, and whatever he perceives & hears he perverts into the substance of his delirious vision (*CL* I:257).

[51] Bald shows how Coleridge's use of the word "Reverie" involves his sensations with opium and his thinking on associations of thought: "In reverie, then, some of the usual barriers are down, and the restraints imposed by reality are no longer heeded. The mind, relaxing its controls, is sometimes a participant, sometimes spectator.... In reverie — day-dream, nightmare, or opium vision — the mind does not insist that successive thoughts and images should have all the 'necessary

connections' by which they 'produce each other in the world of reality'"
("Addenda" 40).

⁵² Patricia M. Adair develops the theme of confused waking and dream worlds,
suggesting, "There are moments in *The Ancient Mariner* when the two worlds
mesh, and, through the power of imagination, the outer world becomes the inner":
The Waking Dream: A Study of Coleridge's Poetry (London: Edward Arnold,
1969) 92-93. See also Edward Bostetter, "The Nightmare World of *The Ancient
Mariner*," *Studies in Romanticism* I (1962): 241-54.

⁵³ McGann *Critique* 60.

⁵⁴ This is McElderry's reading, evidenced by his statement on the revisions of
Parts V and VI that "Coleridge himself admits the justness of the criticism that the
poem was in this central section confused and over long. Since all of these changes
are demonstrably for the better it is time that the reviewers be given some belated
credit for contributing to the improvement of a poem so original that it must have
baffled a merely conventional taste. Incidentally, it is pleasant to think that
Coleridge was not too hyper-sensitive to profit from plain-spoken criticism" (78-
79).

⁵⁵ For the influence of opium addiction on "The Ancient Mariner," see
especially Bald, "Addenda" 26-45. For Coleridge's religious and philosophical
views, see Thomas McFarland, *Coleridge and the Pantheist Tradition* (Oxford:
The Clarendon P, 1969); and Raimonda Modiano, *Coleridge and the Concept of
Nature* (Tallahassee: Florida State UP, 1985).

⁵⁶ Campbell 597.

⁵⁷ See my article, "Return and Representation: The Revisions of 'The Ancient
Mariner,'" *The Wordsworth Circle* 17 (1986): 148-56, on the revisions of quotation
marks and other details that conspire to form a significant narration over and
beyond what the Mariner tells the Wedding Guest.

⁵⁸ In a letter to Biggs and Cottle concerning the second edition of *Lyrical
Ballads*, Wordsworth writes of the "Antient Mariner" (*EY* 303). In only one edition
does this same spelling appear, and that is the 1805, at line 77. As Coleridge
nowhere uses this spelling, we can conjecture that Wordsworth alone supervised
the publication of the poem in 1805.

⁵⁹ McGann raises a similar concern in regard to Canto 3 of Byron's *Don Juan*,
which was copied — and somewhat altered — by Mary Shelley: *Critique* 43, 52-53.

[60] See Paul Magnuson, *Coleridge and Wordsworth: A Lyrical Dialogue* (Princeton: Princeton UP, 1988); Modiano, *Coleridge and the Concept of Nature* 33-50; Thomas McFarland, *Romanticism and the Forms of Ruin: Wordsworth, Coleridge, and Modalities of Fragmentation* (Princeton: Princeton UP, 1981) 56-108; William Heath, *Wordsworth and Coleridge* (Oxford: Oxford UP, 1970). But also see Stephen Maxfield Parrish, *The Art of the Lyrical Ballads* (Cambridge, Mass.: Harvard UP, 1973) 34-79; and Buchan, "The Influence of Wordsworth on Coleridge."

[61] Raimonda Modiano focusses on this interruption to trace the Wedding-Guest's impact on the poem: "Words and 'Languageless' Meanings: Limits of Expression in The Rime of the Ancient Mariner" *Modern Language Quarterly* 38 (1977): 40-61. Modiano distinguishes "two modes of language" in the Mariner's narration which disclose an inherent struggle in his understanding. According to Modiano's dichotomy, the Mariner recounts his experiences most directly "in a language that is primarily sensorial and concrete," and he speaks with others "in a language that does not record objects but assigns them meanings dependent upon a system of shared mythology" (51-52). As he struggles with his narration, and becomes increasingly aware of a need to communicate his memory to his auditor, the Mariner succumbs to the language of social discourse, and eventually "identifies himself completely with the public values represented by his auditor" (52). Modiano's argument thus shows how the process of appropriation works at yet another level.

[62] *CN* II:2880n.

[63] See Bald's discussion on the notebook entry in connection with the reveries of Coleridge's opium addiction in "Addenda" 33-35.

[64] Lowes 164-68.

[65] Kathleen M. Wheeler, *The Creative Mind in Coleridge's Poetry* (Cambridge, Mass.: Harvard UP, 1981) 50. Wheeler's entire discussion of "The Ancient Mariner" focusses on the addition of the gloss (42-64). Bald also makes the point of the early composition of the gloss ("Addenda" 13).

[66] Bald, "The Ancient Mariner" 528.

[67] Bald, "The Ancient Mariner" 528.

[68] Huntington Brown, in "The Gloss to The Rime of the Ancient Mariner," *Modern Language Quarterly* 6 (1945), playfully submits that the verse is sung by

a pre-Shakespearean minstrel, while "the gloss can only be the work of an imaginary editor . . . . a scholar, modern rather than medieval, but distinctly old fashioned" (320).

[69] *Table Talk* I:274.

[70] Jean-Pierre Mileur traces the distance between the verse narration and the gloss, in *Vision and Revision: Coleridge's Art of Immanence* (Berkeley: U of California P, 1982) 67-74.

[71] Campbell 96.

[72] Campbell 597.

[73] Richard Garnett, ed., *Poetry of Samuel Taylor Coleridge* (New York, 1898) 285.

[74] Lowes 192.

[75] For a thorough account of the neoplatonic structure of the gloss's redaction, see James Twitchell, "The World above the Ancient Mariner," *Texas Studies in Language and Literature* 17 (1975): 103-17; J. B. Beer, *Coleridge the Visionary* (London: Chatto and Windus, 1959) 134-74; and, of course, Piper.

[76] Sarah Dyck, in "Perspective in 'The Ancient Mariner,'" *Studies in English Literature* 13(1973): 591-604, employs the narrative personalities of the verse-minstrel and the gloss-editor suggested by Huntington Brown, to argue that the difference between the Mariner's narration and the gloss's is that between "vital experience" and "intellectual experience" (603). Dyck's discussion provides a valuable account for the Mariner's piously moral ending.

[77] McGann makes this point very clear when he argues that by ignoring the effects of ideology, criticism merely re-enacts the claims imposed by the ideology: "the literary criticism of the 'Rime' has never been, in the proper sense, critical of the poem but has merely recapitulated, in new and various ways, and not always very consciously, what Coleridge himself had polemically maintained" ("The Meaning of The Ancient Mariner" 57). For an account of such recapitulation at work in the most influential discussion of Coleridge's poem, see my "Re-enactment as Reclamation in *The Road to Xanadu,*" *The Journal of Narrative Technique* 17 (1987): 259-72.

Selected Bibliography

Adair, Patricia M. *The Waking Dream: A Study of Coleridge's Poetry*. London: Edward Arnold, 1967.

Bald, R. C. "The Ancient Mariner." *Times Literary Supplement* 26 July 1934: 528.

_____. "Coleridge and the Ancient Mariner: Addenda to the *Road to Xanadu*." *Nineteenth Century Studies*. Ed. Herbert Davis, William C. DeVane and R. C. Bald. Ithaca: Cornell UP, 1940. 1-45.

Beer, John. *Coleridge the Visionary*. London: Chatto and Windus, 1959.

Bostetter, Edward. "The Nightmare of 'The Ancient Mariner'." *Studies in Romanticism* 1 (1962): 241-54.

Brett, R. L., and A. R. Jones, eds. *Wordsworth and Coleridge: The Lyrical Ballads*. London: Methuen, 1965.

Brown, Huntington. "The Gloss to The Rime of the Ancient Mariner." *Modern Language Quarterly* 6 (1945): 319-24.

Buchan, A. M. "The Influence of Wordsworth on Coleridge." *University of Toronto Quarterly* 32 (1963): 346-66.

Coleridge, Samuel Taylor. *Biographia Literaria*. Ed. James Engell and W. Jackson Bate. 2 vols. Vol. 7 of *The Collected Works of Samuel Taylor Coleridge*. Gen. Eds. Kathleen Coburn, and Bart Winer. Princeton: Princeton UP, 1983.

_____. *Collected Letters of Samuel Taylor Coleridge*. Ed. Earl Leslie Griggs. 6 vols. Oxford: The Clarendon P, 1956-71.

_____. *The Complete Poetical and Dramatic Works of Samuel Taylor Coleridge*. Ed. James Dykes Campbell. London: Macmillan, 1893.

_____. *The Notebooks of Samuel Taylor Coleridge*. Ed. Kathleen Coburn. 4 vols. to date. Princeton: Princeton UP, 1957—.

_____. *The Poems of Samuel Taylor Coleridge*. Ed. Derwent and Sara Coleridge. London: Edward Moxon, 1852.

_____. *Poetical Works*. Ed. E. H. Coleridge. Oxford: Oxford UP, 1912.

_____. *Poetry of Samuel Taylor Coleridge*. Ed. Richard Garnett. New York: Charles Scribner's Sons, 1898.

_____. *Table Talk*. 2 vols. Ed. Carl Woodring. Vol. 14 of *The Collected Works* . Princeton: Princeton UP, 1990.

Daniel, R. W. "The Publication of *Lyrical Ballads*." *Modern Language Review* 22 (1938): 406-10.

Empson, William, and David Pirie, eds. *Coleridge's Verse: A Selection*. London: Faber and Faber, 1972.

Forstner, Lorne. "Coleridge's 'The Ancient Mariner' and the Case for Justifiable 'Mythocide': An Argument on Psychological, Epistemological and Formal Grounds." *Criticism* 18 (1976): 211-29.

Foxon, D. F. "The Printing of *Lyrical Ballads*, 1798." *The Library* 5th ser. 9 (1954): 241-41.

Gill, Stephen. *William Wordsworth: A Life*. Oxford: The Clarendon P, 1989.

Hill, John Spencer. *A Coleridge Companion: An Introduction to the Major Poems and the Biographia Literaria*. New York: Macmillan, 1984.

Holmes, Richard. *Coleridge: Early Visions*. New York: Penguin, 1989.

Johnson, Mary Lynn. "How Rare Is a 'Unique Annotated Copy' of Coleridge's *Sibylline Leaves*?" *Bulletin of the New York Public Library* 78 (1975): 451-81.

Jordan, John E. *Why the Lyrical Ballads? The Background, Writing, and Character of Wordsworth's 1798 Lyrical Ballads*. Berkeley: U of California P, 1976.

Lipking, Lawrence. "The Marginal Gloss." *Critical Inquiry* 3 (1977): 609-55.

Lowes, John Livingston. *The Road to Xanadu: A Study in the Ways of the Imagination*. Boston: Houghton Mifflin, 1927.

Magnuson, Paul. *Coleridge and Wordsworth: A Lyrical Dialogue*. Princeton: Princeton UP, 1988.

Mayo, Robert. "The Contemporaneity of the Lyrical Ballads." *Publications of the Modern Language Association* 69 (1954): 486-522.

McElderry, B. R., Jr. "Coleridge's Revisions of 'The Ancient Mariner.'" *Studies in Philology* 29 (1932): 68-94.

McFarland, Thomas. *Coleridge and the Pantheist Tradition*. Oxford: Oxford

UP, 1969.

_____. *Romanticism and the Forms of Ruin: Wordsworth, Coleridge, and Modalities of Fragmentation*. Princeton: Princeton UP, 1981.

McGann, Jerome. *A Critique of Modern Textual Interpretation*. Chicago: U of Chicago P, 1983.

_____. "The Meaning of the 'Ancient Mariner'" *Critical Inquiry* 8 (1981): 35-67.

Mileur, Jean-Pierre. *Vision and Revision: Coleridge's Art of Immanence*. Berkeley: U of California P, 1982.

Modiano, Raimonda. *Coleridge and the Concept of Nature*. Tallahassee: Florida State UP, 1985.

_____. "Words and 'Languageless' Meanings: Limits of Expression in The Rime of the Ancient Mariner." *Modern Language Quarterly* 38 (1977): 40-61.

Owen, W. J. B., ed. *Wordsworth and Coleridge: Lyrical Ballads*. Oxford: Oxford UP, 1967.

Parrish, Stephen Maxfield. *The Art of the Lyrical Ballads*. Cambridge, Mass.: Harvard UP, 1973.

Payne, Richard. "The Style and Spirit of the Elder Poets: 'The Ancient Mariner' and English Literary Tradition." *South Atlantic Quarterly* 41 (1981): 16-26.

Piper, Herbert Walker. *The Active Universe: Pantheism and the Concept of Imagination in the English Romantic Poets*. London: The Athlone P, 1962.

Reed, Mark L. "Wordsworth, Coleridge, and the 'Plan' of the *Lyrical Ballads*." *University of Toronto Quarterly* 34 (1965): 238-53.

Reiman, Donald, ed. *The Romantics Reviewed: Contemporary Reviews of British Romantic Writers*. 9 vols. New York: Garland, 1972.

Stempel, Daniel. "Coleridge's Magical Realism: A Reading of The Rime of the Ancient Mariner." *Mosaic* 12 (1978): 143-56.

Dyck, Sarah. "Perspective in 'The Rime of the Ancient Mariner'" *Studies in English Literature* 13 (1973): 591-604.

Twitchell, James. "The World Above the Ancient Mariner." *Texas Studies in*

Language and Literature 17 (1975): 103-17.

Wallen, Martin. "Re-enactment as Reclamation in The Road toXanadu." The *Journal of Narrative Technique* 17 (1987): 259-272.

_____. "Return and Representation: The Revisions of 'The Ancient Mariner.'" *The Wordsworth Circle* 17 (1986): 148-56.

Warren, Robert Penn. "A Poem of Pure Imagination: An Experiment in Reading." *Selected Essays.* New York: Random House. 198-305.

Wheeler, Kathleen M. *The Creative Mind in Coleridge's Poetry.* Cambridge, Mass.: Harvard UP, 1981.

Wordsworth, William. *Memoirs of William Wordsworth.* London, 1851.

_____. *The Prose Works of William Wordsworth.* Ed. W. J. B. Owen and Jane Worthington Smyser. 3 vols. Oxford: The Clarendon P, 1974.

Wordsworth, William and Dorothy. *The Letters of William and Dorothy Wordsworth: The Early Years, 1787-1805.* Ed. Ernest De Selincourt. Oxford: The Clarendon P, 1967.